THE *BEST* OF ME
THE EMPOWERMENT CHAPTER

By Latonia Francois

Inspiration You Can Write On

Let's Write Life inspirational journals bring together your personal writing and life-guided journaling prompts that will empower you to express yourself, ignite a positive understanding of who you are, and motivate you to fearlessly explore the possibilities of your life. Let this journal nurture your mental health and serve as an inspirational tool, gift, and keepsake that will last far beyond words.

Explore more at **www.LetsWriteLife.com**

"The Best of Me" Guided Journal

Latonia Francois
Trailblazing Owner of Let's Write Life
You're Worth Writing For.

For bulk journal orders, speaking events, and programs, contact the publisher by email at Orders@LetsWritelife.com.

YOUR JOURNEY OF EMPOWERMENT STARTS NOW

ISBN:978-0-9963958-1-6 (hc)
ISBN:978-0-9963958-0-9 (e)

Because of the dynamic nature of the internet, any web addresses, links, or QR Codes included in this journal may have been changed after publication and may no longer be valid. Refer back to LetsWriteLife.com for all on-line resources and information.

Designed by: H&L Imprints Graphic Design & Photo, HLImprints.com
Printed in the United States of America

FIRST EDITION: JUNE 2015, 35C
FIRST EDITION REPRINTED: AUG 2015, 100C
SECOND EDITION, PLANNED TO REPRINT: JUNE 2016, 1000C
FIRST EDITION, REPRINTED WITH UPDATES: AUGUST 2017, 50C

LET'S **Write** LIFE™
by Latonia Francois
YOU'RE WORTH WRITING FOR.
FOR MORE JOURNALS: WWW.LETSWRITELIFE.COM
@letswritelife

Surround yourself with people who believe in your dreams...

I dedicate this journal to the imprints in my life that empowered me to chose happiness and live a life of joy; my love Herkins, my little peanut Kyra, and my little munch munch Desiree. Thank you to my parents, sister, brother, and close friends who all continue to believe in me and support my dreams. You all make this worth it.

With joy, I especially dedicate this journal to everyday survivors who have overcome so many challenges and are still going strong. This is also to those who need light in a dark place to know their potential. Let this journal not only represent you, but bring light to the aspects of your life that truly **BRING OUT** the **BEST** of **YOU!**

With you I share my joy.

Be Strong and Courageous

9 Have I not commanded you? Be strong and courageous. Do not be afraid; do not be discouraged, for the Lord your God will be with you wherever you go. *Joshua 1:9*

What's My Story?

LET'S = Together We Can

WRITE = Make Real

LIFE = What's Most Meaningful to Us

Let's Write Life means how we can "make real", or bring to reality, everything in our life that is most meaningful to us. I've always loved encouraging others, helping them achieve their goals, and seeing that they become the person I always knew they could be. Since they don't always believe in themselves, I wanted to share with them an aspect of my life that has empowered me. Let's Write Life brings together everything in our lives that empowers us and teaches us more about who we are and what we aspire to be through a personal use of journaling. Encouraging others is embedded in who I am and I'm excited that I can be apart of your journey to greatness through journaling!

Let's Write Life was birthed out of my desire to transform my life in a meaningful way. It took a rock bottom situation to motivate me to choose happiness with everything that was in me and overcome the challenges that I faced. I began a journey that brought me through some of the best and most difficult times in my life. It is my life story that I now share as encouragement with many people through journaling, because I know what it feels like to be stuck and lose sight of how to get from where you are to where you desire to be. It is my mission to guide you with specific and unique journaling techniques that you can use effectively as you pursue a transformational life journey of your own.

Every Let's Write Life journal, retreat, and event represents a different chapter in my life to share the many pieces of my story and how journaling empowered me along the way. These are my stories I share to encourage you and to lift you up. Let each piece of my story be the push you need to look inwardly to discover more about who you are, your life, and present everyday joy. In this chapter of my life, entitled "The Best of Me", is how I began living to discover joy from the inside out through the people, experiences, and everything that brings out the best of me.

Let's open this chapter...

"THE BEST OF ME"

My Life. My Story. Everything that brings out the best of me.

How do you breakaway from feeling stuck in a rut in your life? How do you face life challenges without giving up? How do you relieve stress from work, drama with friends, family life, or relationships when you don't have a way to escape the chaos of life? When money is an issue, where do you find the reassurance that everything will be okay? How do you heal from a broken past or a traumatic life event that has shook your world? How do you move beyond a state of anger, depression, suicidal thoughts, tragedy, health matters, or any current setback to see that you can overcome them? Do you know what makes your life worth fighting for? What purpose, what journey, what joys in life bring out the best of you? My hope is that my story will inspire you to explore journaling in a whole new way that transforms your life.

From a young age I've had a history of suffering with depression brought on by broken relationships, traumatic life events, grief, rejection, verbal abuse, and unforgiveness with family, friends, and people who judged me without knowing me at all. All of these issues I suppressed over the years, holding hurt and pain deep inside. I use to isolate myself thinking no one cared about me or that I had to always keep it together in order to prevent being judged or written off. My self-esteem and confidence in myself was low. The fear of being rejected and judged by people I cared about made me feel extremely ashamed. Masks became the reflection of my pain. I wore masks to show people around me that I was okay. Wearing masks made me believe I could live up to everyone's expectations. It seemed easier to be who I thought everyone wanted me to be rather than be myself. I moved forward through life believing all those suppressed feelings would disappear. Journaling became my voice to vent out the words that illustrated my unspoken pain. Throughout my teenage years and into my adulthood it became my lifestyle to conceal my depression, to journal, and to brush all of my past wounds under a rug.

In 2013, I found myself in the midst of depression that had reared its head in my life once again. This time was different. I was running my first business for seven years and raising a growing family. I was also pregnant with my second daughter; a time of joy. Unfortunately, all sorts of transitions were taking place with my business and personal life. As a result, all the vast changes were leading to devastating financial issues. At the same time, I was having difficulty dealing with a few long-term relationships with people I could no longer deal with. I wanted these relationships restored or brought to a mutually peaceful end. The amount of stress overwhelmed me and I found myself facing the same deep-rooted pains of my past. These issues stirred up feelings of anxiety and sadness inside of me that had been fighting to be freed. I was tired of it all. At the pit of my soul, I felt hurt and alone. I had a desperate cry on my heart to be happy, because for a long time I was not.

Day by day, I was lost in the frustration of my emotions not knowing what to do. As I had always done, I began journaling about all the thoughts on my mind. How these issues took place and how I wished they all would stop fueled my writing. I wished I could be happy for a change. Every emotion I felt filled the lines of my journal as I began to think:

- If my current situation never changed, how could I move forward with meaningful joy in the midst of my pain?
- How could I let go of the silent depression that imprisoned me?
- If I never made any more money than what I'm making today or live the lifestyle I want, how could I live with joy, right now, even in the midst of my pain?
- How could I "make real" this life of happiness I thought about?

I was tired of chasing life, tired of trying to be accepted, and tired of trying to fit into the unrealistic expectations everyone put on me. Moving forward and ignoring the issues that bothered me only made me feel worse. It was killing me inside to not spend more of my life living free from depression, a broken past, and negative thoughts that made me feel stuck. How could I make my life worth living for without the fear of rejection, sadness, or shame of failing affect me? I was desperate to found out.

My curiosities led me on a journey. On that journey there were many ups and downs. Changes that were happening made me feel inspired. I moved full speed ahead, but I soon realized the changes I wanted were not all happening in my life the way I expected them to be. I was still dealing with the same preexisting challenges with work, money, and stress of life all around me. I was no longer working on a regular basis due to difficulties with my pregnancy. Guilt of not being able to financially support my family made me feel like I was losing everything; all that I worked for and everything that I loved was falling apart. Even my attempts to mend broken relationships, that I wanted restored, turned into hurtful experiences. I wanted my family members and friends to understand how their relationships were hurting me, because I cared about them so much. A broken part of me wanted them to understand my struggles; be there for me in this time. The outcomes of trying to talk to them were not the results I had hoped for. Dealing with all the situations that were changing for the worse consumed me. The burden of stress made me want to give up and let it all go.

Feeling myself shifting down into depression that I knew all to well, all I could think about were these words that spoke loudly in the back of my mind saying, "No. Not this time. I won't be defeated. I'm not giving up. I want to be happy." My mind refused to accept the latch of my past with depression creeping back in. An urge of anger came over me and I rejected the painful thoughts. No more could I let the struggles I was facing continue to control me. I had been in that place of silent pain for too long and too many times before. I thought, "This is my life and I have to make a choice. The life I desire for myself and my family depends on me moving forward." I hit a wall of frustration and said, "Enough is enough. I am not going to be hindered by these things or let them steal my joy, time, or energy anymore."

A TURNING POINT

Seeking an outlet to pour out my tears and the waves of emotions that built up inside, I grabbed my journal and began writing the flood of frustrations I needed to let go. I spent days earnestly writing about the thoughts weighing on my mind. Thoughts I had of being happy became stronger the more I wrote through my pain. I could feel how much seeking my own happiness meant to me. Once and for all I wanted to be happy. Not the surface level of happiness that I was accustomed to showing through a masked smile everyday, but happiness fueled by joy within my heart. I wanted to be happy and to think about something other than pain; anything to help me pull my mind away from being depressed.

My oldest daughter Kyra's birthday had recently passed and I thought about the memory of that day. Thinking about it made me smile. It was a day filled with dress-up princess clothes for Kyra, a bike ride through the city park, and a night of quality family time for just her, dad, and me with the presence of Desiree growing in my belly. That memory gave me joy. I grabbed my phone, so I could watch the memory I captured from that day. Kyra had recently started to spell her first name; which I made sure I recorded in that video. She made me feel so proud. Kyra reminded me I was loved. I felt I had given her a great birthday even though I could not afford to buy her anything or take her out to a kid's party place. Everything worked out. It was my proud mommy moment. She didn't care about our lifestyle, party plans, or issues surrounding me. She was more than happy to simply be with me. It was a day I wanted to remember, because it gave me meaningful joy in the midst of my pain.

From that point on, I realized how powerful the memory of that day was and how it allowed me to see beyond my situation. The memory of that day brought joy to my heart in a simple way. It was the presence of joy I yearned to feel everyday. That joy gave me strength; a piece of me I needed in order to persevere through my darkest times. Realizing this I began spending hours and days writing in my journal about that memory and the life I wanted to have. I wrote about what made me happy, such as: my family, traveling, goals I had for myself, living life no longer afraid to try new things, and so much more. I desired to let go of my past, to be confident in who I was, and face life's challenges with the strength I needed to overcome them. I was certain, "I never want to let the same issues continue to steal my joy ever again. Right now, I want to be happy. I'm choosing happiness for me."

Writing about my joys and pains was a new experience. I wrote about events from my past that hurt me and the joy I wanted to help me move forward. Journaling allowed me to reflect, express myself, and my thoughts as I moved forward working to make changes in my life. I had to face people I loved, personal fears, and hurtful situations that terrified me. I did not want to face these challenges, but I knew facing them meant my life would change. As I went through each experience, I learned I was holding onto pain for so long. I had no idea that pain had turned into anger and that anger had turned into unforgiveness that I needed to let go. Painful situations I faced as a young girl were now the root of many challenges I was facing in my adult life. Writing about these situations gave me a new perspective. I now wrote about these events from a point of healing and with the positive outlook I now had.

Journaling was no longer venting for me. It was a journey through journaling I was experiencing to change my life. This journey allowed me to see beyond my challenges and discover the things in my life that answered those questions I asked myself, at the start of my journey, in order to discover what meaningful joy meant to me. What did it mean for me to be happy? The memory of Kyra's birthday gave me joy and put my life and the things that mattered into perspective for me to answer that question. I was able to see my way through life's challenges and discover the joy I desired through people, prayer, and experiences that reflected what happiness meant to me. Every time I felt discouraged, burdened with stress, or overwhelmed I would look through my journal and every time I wrote in it I felt like I could keep moving forward another day, overcome any setbacks, and face life with a new purpose. My written words gave me joy, motivation, and a positive mindset to change the life around me. Journaling about my own happiness and discovering what it meant brought out The Best of Me.

As I continued journaling, I reflected over aspects of my life within the pages of my writing as proof that I had overcome my past with depression and was able to let go of so much hurt. I discovered that the joy I was looking for, I already had. Going through those past experiences that once affected me negatively, I now used those experiences as fuel to become "The Best of Me". I realized my self-worth and how much my kids, my family, and my future meant to me. Journaling became the tool to visualize meaningful aspects of my life and to not take my life for granted due to setbacks. My writing helped me see what joy looked liked for myself and I began aligning my life with my goals, meaningful people, experiences, and everything I loved being apart of it.

Here's What I Learned

I learned that the joy I desired, I already had; not because the life around me changed, but because I DID. I made a decision to choose happiness. How I felt about myself mattered much more than my circumstance and the opinions of others. I learned to take responsibility for my own joy, uncover the issues I feared, and rely on faith to face the impossible. I did not give up on my journey. As I faced each challenge, I made journaling a tool of empowerment to help me move forward. My joy came when I made a decision to look inwardly and start transforming my life from the inside out as I pushed forward to continue my journey. What I discovered was "The Best of Me."

I Share My Joy With You

What was just a cry on my heart to be happy has become my life-changing journey of discovering joy, knowing my self-worth, and pursuing my passion to encourage others through journaling. It was very hard to see the life I was capable of living, because it looked too hard from where I was standing. My personal use of journaling is what worked for me. When I began to step out and not give up on what I wanted, the life I desired appeared. I'm still on this journey, but now I'm on it to encourage you!

I created "THE BEST OF ME" to capture the essence of this significant chapter of my life. "THE BEST OF ME" is not about pouring out your past into a journey where nothing changes. "THE BEST OF ME" represents the journey forward to a life not defined by your past. It is about discovering the joy you have found for yourself through the people, experiences, the good and bad times, your spiritual journey, and whatever you choose to bring happiness into your life today. These are the positive aspects of your life that you would not be the same without. The memories, stories, and positive life changes that BRING OUT the best of you.

I have structured this journal in a way that will expand your mind to journaling and allow you to explore your life in a meaningful way. Let this journal be a space that encourages you, empowers you to choose happiness, and discover the things in your life that truly allow you to let "IT" go, whatever "IT" might be. This is a new step towards living a life based on who you truly are. Allow yourself the freedom to understand what it means for YOU to be happy. LIVE in a way that feels great to YOU. I'm putting the emphasis on YOU because for many years, I let the expectations of others, hurtful relationships, and certain life events dictate the way I thought I wanted to live my life. You can do this. You can be strong. This time it is about YOU and your choices. It is time to see the things in your life that will pull you through.

"Life is not just about living, but a journey of experiencing, loving, and discovering the best of who you are."   -Latonia

In my journal I captured pictures, inspirational quotes, uplifting scriptures, art journaling, and my best-kept memories that made me smile. My journal captured The Best of Me; a place I captured my memories, my story, and dreams of the life I desired. As I captured the many unsung aspects of my life I saw the type of woman I had become and the things in my life that have shaped me into the person I am today. Seeing my life in this way made me stronger and I began to heal from the hurt I held onto for so long. I began letting go of hurt from my past and I discovered my true ability to keep moving forward.

This Best of Me Life Journal is a place for you to capture memories, embrace new beginnings, and see the things in your life that bring out the best of you. Let this journal be a source of empowerment to be with you when there is no one to reach out to. Capture the many pieces of your unique journey. These are the people, experiences, and everything that brings you joy and because they do, **they will** bring out the Best of You!

THE BEST OF ME

My life is a story I share to ignite a light of hope in your life. With my team, it is through the lives we are able to touch every single day and around the world that guides us to create journals and writing tools of empowerment to be with you on your journey through journaling. We believe, "You're worth writing for." You always were. You always will be!

Let's Write Life,

Follow Hashtag
#MyBestofMe on Instagram to join
The Best of Me Journey.

WELCOME
The Best of Me

It's time to explore journaling and create a journal of empowerment that encourages you to celebrate your life victories, embrace new beginnings, and capture the simplest aspects of your life that gives you hope and joy. This journal is designed to teach you about journaling and how to make it an empowering aspect of your daily life. You will learn a lot, so allow yourself time to take it all in. Move at your own pace.

Life is full of ups and downs. Let this journal be your light in a dark place. Let it remind you of what's important to you. Let it remind you that you are not a failure and you can overcome life challenges. You can stand against your opposition in the midst of tough times, because you are a survivor! Here, you will see beyond your trials, write about where you have been, and how you have already overcome!

This journal represents the best of you and new beginnings for your next chapter. Be empowered by the words you write.

Your Story. Your Way.

The following pages are dedicated to showcase every aspect of your life that's meaningful to you.

What you will find:

- A Self-Reflection Letter
- Relax. Live. Create. Journaling Activities
- QR Code Journal Tags for Interactive Journaling
- Lined and Blank Pages for Journaling

Every aspect of your life, good or bad, has shaped you into the person you are today. How you move forward makes the difference. -Latonia

MY BEST ME
Manifesto

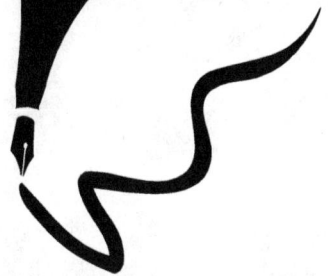

THIS JOURNAL REPRESENTS THE BEST OF ME.

Life, love, and joy by my terms. This is what matters most. It is my life in my own words: what I believe, what success means to me, and what makes my life meaningful. Today, I choose happiness. The depth of my joy exist in being grateful for what I already have and what I believe will be achieved through me. I exhale all my stress and worry. I am not defined by my past. I am moving forward with confidence to achieve my wildest dreams beyond what I can see. I will turn my pain into power. I will stop letting fear win. It's time to let "it" go and welcome new beginnings. I am on a journey of loving who I am, accepting love, and showing love to others. I am blessed and not broken. I have a purpose that the world needs.

TODAY, I AM THE BEST OF ME.

My name is _____ and this is my story.
Started _____. This is my empowering journey to discovering The Best of Me.

LET'S *Write* LIFE™
by Latonia Francois
YOU'RE WORTH WRITING FOR.

Life lessons teach lessons.

-Latonia

GETTING STARTED
INTRODUCTION

A LETTER TO MY BEST ME

This is an opportunity for you to spend time letter writing. Let this letter of self-expression be written with words, art journaling, images, quotes, and all the things that will inspire you to start moving forward in the direction of your life goals and big dreams. Ask yourself, what comes next? What do you want to do with your life? What truly matters to you? This letter represents a blank canvas of your life. It is waiting to be filled with the opening words to begin your journey through journaling.

Spend this time reflecting on everything in your life that has shaped who you are today and how you plan to move forward. Don't limit yourself. Express your goals, dreams, or how you desire to make an impact in the world. Imagine what your new beginning would look like if you could start over today. This is your fresh start.

PROUD MOMMY MOMENT

This journal opens with my story. It took falling into a rock bottom place, before I was able to look up, stop, and take time to evaluate the status of my life. Journaling helped me see beyond my current situation. My desire was to see more of the things in my life that made me happy. In my story, I talked about a memory that helped me see past my pain. It was the memory of Kyra I had recorded on my phone at a time I felt I had lost everything. This video I watched from my phone marks that very meaningful moment that transformed journaling for me and the way I chose to live my life.

Watch Video: **My Proud Mommy Moment**
Scan QR Code or Visit the Link: **http://goo.gl/i5CBKT**

DEDICATED TO:

What is that moment for you? What moment marked the start of your journey to start rewrite your life? As you go through life, never forget that meaningful thought, memory, or person that empowered you to change your life. It is in the remembrance of your past that you truly find gratitude in seeing how far you've come.

FEELING STUCK

Not sure what things bring joy to your life? Do you feel unhappy with challenges you are facing right now? Is there pain and hurt you want removed from your life?

Use this time to express how you feel about your life and your future. Thinking about your life ahead will help you see beyond your current situation. Every aspect of your life, both good and bad, has shaped you into the person you are today. How you move forward makes the difference. Let this letter be used in a positive way to describe who you are and give your writing journey a fresh start by reflecting on your life and all the people, places, and everything that empowers you.

To begin, write about what you would like to change in your life to experience the joy you desire. Then make a list of five goals you wish to achieve in your life. Don't limit yourself and don't worry about how you will achieve them, just focus on writing whatever is on your heart. Bring your awareness to any negative thoughts. Challenge negative thoughts with positive words that speak life and joy over sadness. Your voice matters. You deserve to be happy!

Here are some helpful writing ideas:

Start by stating:

- Right now I don't feel joy in my life, but what would make me feel better is…
- My life would be different if I could…
- The things in my life that I wish would change are…
- I feel my best when…
- My experience with _____ impacted my life in ways that hurt me, but I will not let it define me. Here are three reasons I will try to keep moving forward and not give up on being the person I know I can be.
  1._____ 2._____, 3._____.

Writing what you feel today will give you a glimpse at the things in your life you can take steps to change, achieve, or overcome. Every time you feel down or overwhelmed by life challenges, come back to this letter space and remember why you held on so long in the first place. Focus on writing more about the life you desire in a positive way to help you see beyond what you may be facing right now. Let this be the first step you take towards living a life you desire. You can make the choice.

DEDICATED TO:

Dedicate this space to visualize what matters most to you, life goals, and big dreams.
PHOTOS. WRITTEN WORDS. ART JOURNALING. QUOTES. POEMS. SONGS.

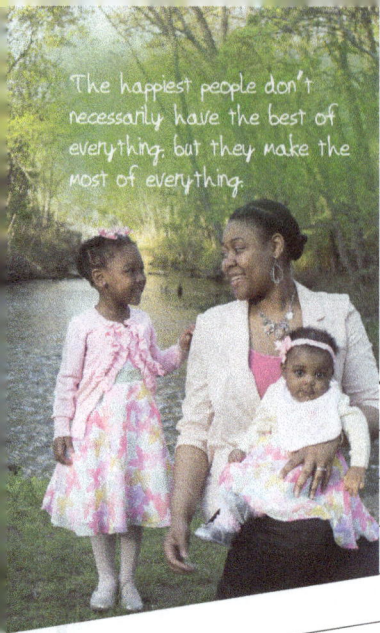
The happiest people don't necessarily have the best of everything, but they make the most of everything.

A LETTER TO MY BEST ME.

Express who you are and what things in your life bring out the BEST OF YOU.

/   /

/   /

Your Desire to Change Must be **GREATER THAN** Your Desire to Stay the Same.

Life's not about how fast you reach the finish line, it's about making the most of your journey along the way.

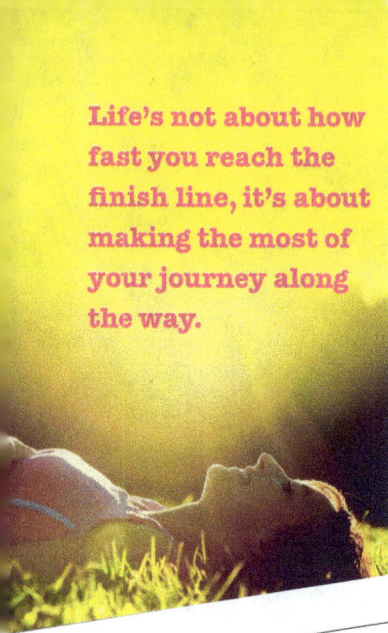

/   /

Those with the confidence to move forward past the obstacles of life will look back one day and say, look how far I've come.

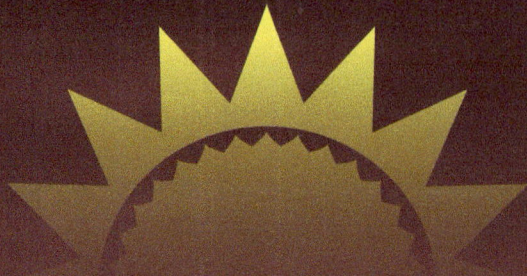

TODAY, I CHOOSE HAPPINESS.

I MADE IT MY CHOICE.

NO MATTER THE CIRCUMSTANCE,

I DESIRE TO LIVE IN JOY.

MY LIFE HAS NEW MEANING.

MY PAST CAN NOT STAY.

I WILL NOT BE DEFEATED.

I WILL NOT BE PERSUADED.

TODAY, I CHOOSE HAPPINESS.

THERE IS NO OTHER WAY.

- LATONIA FRANCOIS

RELAX.

LIVE.

CREATE.

Empowerment, confidence, and the freedom to be who you truly are…all wrapped in the great benefits of journaling. While you're creating this awesome journal, I want to expand your mind to a few journaling techniques you can incorporate into your journaling experience.

JOURNALING LESSONS:

RELAX. Exploring Journaling to Relax

LIVE. Making Journaling A Lifestyle

CREATE. Art Journaling You Can Picture

RELAX. LIVE. CREATE.
LESSON ONE

There are many benefits to journaling that can improve your overall well-being. Journaling to relax is at the top of my list! Let's start by talking about the basics of journaling.

WHAT IS JOURNALING?
Journaling is a personal record of self-expression through written words and art that relate to the innermost thoughts, events, and reflections of your life. Depending on your personal preference, you may chose to write in a daily journal or keep a journal over certain periods of time.

WHY JOURNAL?
Journaling provides a solution to mental and emotional needs, and your overall psychological well-being. It clears your mind, relieves stress, and records the events of your life. I like to simplify this answer into two categories of reasoning: to be reactive and proactive to emotional needs. Below I have listed a few examples.

Reactive: Self-healing to vent, relieve stress, grieve, let out frustrations, instant gratification to escape the chaos of life

Proactive: Personal enrichment for clarity, prioritizing goals, visioning, empowerment, taking control of circumstances

When we do all these things, we are expressing ourselves. Our self-expression is a solution to achieve an emotional need. Journaling is an outlet that helps us release self-expression through writing.

NOW, LET'S EXPLORE JOURNALING IN A WAY THAT'S RELAXING.

To relax is to step into a state of mind in which you are free to LET IT GO! "IT" might be:

- Stress
- Anxiety
- Anger
- Hurt
- A Big Decision
- Issues at Work
- Too Many Obligations

- Financial Hardship
- Responsibilities
- Worry
- Maintaining the Household
- Lack of Confidence
- Unhappiness

- Guilt
- Grief
- Mental Overload
- Broken Relationships
- Life In General
- What's Your "It"?

Sometimes it's just great to take a break from it all. To relax, means that you are putting a PAUSE on life and giving yourself space to just let "IT" go— at least for a moment. Wouldn't it be nice to step into a state of relaxation whenever and wherever you needed to? Well, I'm going to share a little story of mine that I hope will inspire you.

It was two days before Christmas and I had been battling a cold for a few days. I was not feeling my best, so I took some time to sit back and slow things down. I got a call from a friend and our talk made me think about all the stressful transitions I was facing in my life at that time. I began thinking how I hated feeling as though I had no direction for current situations and all the decisions I needed to make seemed like they were all just up in the air. Thinking about everything made me feel as though I was stuck and couldn't move forward.

Out of frustration I began to cry. A downpour of tears began to flood my face, so I went to grab tissues. All of a sudden as I began to wipe the tears from my eyes and release all the emotions I was feeling, my baby girl Desiree (who had been sitting in her high chair eating Cheerios and watching PBS Kids) began to laugh at me. In my mind I was a little confused, because I wasn't sure if this little baby who couldn't yet talk was really laughing at me or something else. She was just so suddenly happy that I believed she thought I was cracking up laughing behind the tissues that were hiding my tears. The more I looked at her, the more she would began smiling and laughing at me. I couldn't understand why. She had the biggest smile on her face and she was laughing so much, that in my crying, all I could think about was how she has always been my sign of joy.

I continued to cry because of everything that was still on my mind and continued to wipe my face of tears. The more I cried the more Desiree laughed. I would take the tissues away from my eyes to see what she was laughing at and she would be smiling at me. I then wiped my face more with my tissues and she would begin to laugh again. I soon figured out what was making Desiree laugh. Every time I put the tissues over my eyes I assume she thought I was playing hide and seek and that is what made her laugh. Every time I put the tissues up to my face she laughed and I began to play this game with her. Inevitably, I was no longer crying, but laughing at the fact that I couldn't cry when I really wanted to. She was my little angel there to cheer me up. I had joy right in front of me.

This story is one of my favorite inspirations, because when I need to relax it reminds me of that moment of joy that unexpectedly helped me put a pause on life when I needed to let "IT" go. I let that experience be my outlook throughout the rest of that day. After laughing with the baby, I began to journal about little Desiree and the moment we shared. I journaled to capture the memory of all that happened and I went on throughout my day with a change of mindset. I no longer had the feeling of being defeated, rather a feeling of freedom and joy. I took a step back and was reminded that everything would be okay.

As I journaled I played music, incorporated scriptures and memories of other experiences that made me happy while journaling. I found a place to write where I felt most comfortable and spent enough time writing that my hand literally hurt. By the time I was done, I felt like I had let out everything I needed to say. I accomplished something. I got the feeling like I just marked something off my to-do list, but most of all I gave myself the space and time I needed to RELAX. I stepped away from what was making me feel down and just relaxed.

In my writing I gained clarity of my thoughts and I saw the bigger picture that everything would be okay. After that day, I continued writing my way through that stressful time in my life with the thoughts of other moments of joy or other things I wanted to do for myself and I would escape the chaos of life through my writing. The more I approached writing with a mindset to let "IT" go, the easier it became for me to journal in a relaxing way. Now, journaling is my daily vacation through writing, my ME time, my time to relax and LET "IT" GO.

To help you relax, consciously be aware that you are going to pause and spend time journaling wherever you feel overwhelmed, stressed, or need peace of mind. Take a look at the "Types of Journals" list in the "LIVE" activity section for ideas. When you approach journaling this way, you're being proactive and have the opportunity to transition into a relaxing state of mind. This takes practice, but it will become easier over time.

The benefit to journaling is that it gives you time to mentally express your thoughts and redirect them in a positive way. Through your writing, you are able to release the intensity of feelings that you hold inside and think beyond yourself to gain clarity of thoughts. By journaling you will feel calmer and better able to stay in the present situation, but with a new outlook.

Our stories may be different, but our approach to journaling can be the same. Here are three proactive tips you can incorporate when you are journaling to relax:

- ## Let "IT" Go
  Redirect your thoughts towards letting go of whatever "it" is. Let "it" go before you write or let "it" go through your writing, so you can release the intensity of whatever you are feeling and find ways to bring inspiration, positive affirmations, or good memories into your thoughts. Focus your thoughts on things that will help you relax.

- ## Set the Atmosphere

  Write in an atmosphere you feel most comfortable in. After all, you are supposed to be relaxing. If being outdoors or staying inside is relaxing for you, go to a place that you love. Play music, get into comfortable clothes, find somewhere you can write undisturbed, and just incorporate anything that helps you feel relaxed and adds an element of joy into this set aside private journaling time.

- ## Let's Write Life

  Relaxing physically and mentally are both equally important. If you need to cry, talk to someone, take a nap, go outside, or draw, do what you need to relieve stress. Once you've resolved your physical needs, take the time journaling to understand and express your emotional needs. Reflect on what caused your need for relaxation. Journaling will help you notice your patterns, so you can identify specific solutions to your needs.

  Don't limit yourself. Give yourself the time you need to relax and express everything on your mind. Don't edit your writing. Write freely. Write about the life you want, the joy you want, and even the thoughts that seem impossible or make no sense at all. For at least 20 minutes or how ever long it takes, write about anything that's on your mind ...and as often as needed.

FEELING STUCK?

If you're stuck, start with open-ended questions like, "How do I feel today?" or since we're talking about relaxing ask yourself, "Where would I like to go that's far away from here and yet brings me the most comfort?" There are no right or wrong answers to these questions. The goal is just for you to write and express everything that's on your mind. Think beyond the questions and write freely.

Whenever you feel stressed, make journaling an outlet to express whatever is on your mind!

THE SUCCESS OF MAKING JOURNALING APART OF YOUR LIFE COMES WHEN YOU DISCOVER YOU CAN WRITE YOUR WAY **THROUGH ANYTHING!**

RELAX. LIVE. CREATE.
LESSON TWO

MAKING JOURNALING A LIFESTYLE

For centuries, journaling has been a private way for people to express themselves, capture memories, or preserve life stories. It's a paper-bound pastime that's deeply rooted in self-expression through writing. When most people think of journaling, they think of keeping a diary or just writing what's on their mind. While those are ways to kept a journal, there are many more benefits. The success with making journaling a part of your life comes when you discover you can write your way through anything!

I love teaching people about journaling and how to discover ways to incorporate it into their lives. From person to person, journaling can start in so many different ways and that's what I love most about it. Without limits, journaling can be whatever you need it to be, whenever you need it. Through it, we can truly capture the innermost thoughts that tell the stories of our lives. The more you journal the more your life unfolds through written words, personal interests, photos, videos, art, and everything that is as unique as the life of the author. Our life is the essence of journaling and there is so much more to journaling when you can enjoy the way you capture your life and the memories of it.

When I was very young I attended Sunday school and I remember one day my teacher doing an activity where all the kids got to decorate composition notebooks to create prayer journals. We all got to customize our own notebooks with stickers, colors, and all the embellishments we wanted. My mom and I use to collect stickers, so I remember being extremely excited when she let me use some to decorate my prayer journal cover. I also had fortune cookie sized paper cutouts of bible verses I received inside of plastic eggs from an Easter egg hunt I attended earlier that year. Having no idea what else I would do with them, I thought it would be a great idea to include those bible verse cutouts on my journal cover. When the decorating was done, I felt like I had created my first masterpiece. I have to say, I think God was very pleased! I even went home and added my own self-made locket for this journal. This was the start to my journaling history and my life story in my own words. My first journal entry started with a prayer.

I was pretty young when I started journaling and believe me, I didn't find a lot to write about as a kid. I certainly wasn't journaling everyday and my journals lasted a whole lot longer than they do now. As I grew up my prayer journal became my daily journal capturing all the great aspects of my life and I began to use it more frequently. As more years passed, my life continued to change. I experienced hurtful relationships as I entered my teenage years and my journaling became an outlet to confide in. It was during this time that journaling became a way to express myself when I didn't feel a connection to others to talk and to say how I was feeling.

As I became an adult and experienced more change in my life, I realized how much journaling had allowed me to think freely, write, and helped me to clearly see the bigger picture in the midst of my good times and my challenges. The more I journaled, the more I become in touch with my inner thoughts, goals, and became more aware of the things that truly mattered to me. I discovered journaling could be so much more than writing in a small notebook, so I decided to give a purpose to all my journaling based on what I wanted to achieve through it. My purpose for journaling expanded into not just being an outlet to express feelings of hurt or daily thoughts as I did in the past, but a source of empowerment capturing meaningful pieces of my life everyday. I began journaling in so many creative ways, personally and professionally, that brought joy into my life and this is what I now share with you.

//

Be the author.
When it comes to your life
story; you hold the pen.

-Latonia **//**

CAPTURE LIFE WHILE IT'S HAPPENING

Journaling is a tool that will empower you to overcome life challenges and captures memories of your life. Once you understand how to effectively use it, then you will be ready to write your way through anything. The ability to achieve your goals and build your dreams lives inside of you. Journaling is just the tool to help you realize it.

I share my history of journaling to show that, in good times and bad, journaling can be whatever you need it to be. Your success with journaling effectively comes when you give a purpose to your writing. What you put in is what you will get out of it. On the following pages, there is a list of benefits to journaling and a list of types of journals to help you think about ways to incorporate journaling into your everyday life in relation to goals you would like to achieve. Take a look over both lists and think about the benefits you wish to achieve through journaling.

- ## Benefits of Journaling

  How do you effectively achieve the benefits of journaling to get the results or healing that you need? I like to use this example, when you go to a gym or want to lose weight, there are certain routines and exercises you must do to achieve your own individual fitness goals. The same routines used to build abs will not prepare you to run a 5K marathon. It's the same with the mind and emotions, there are certain journaling techniques you can apply to achieve different benefits you want to experience. You must start by determining what your purpose for journaling will be and then use certain types of journaling techniques to achieve the results you desire.

- ## Types of Journals

  Once you give your journaling a purpose, try a new type of journal to help you achieve it. On the types of journals list, you can see the variety of journals that exist, including some I've used, to experience the benefits of journaling. What types of journals stand out to you? All the journals listed serve a purpose and allow you to experience the benefits of journaling in various ways.

The more you write, the more you'll discover the way journaling works best for you. From my lifetime evolution of journaling, you can see it's certainly not one size fits all. My journaling changed as much as my life did. It can be whatever you need it to be. Journaling is meant to fit YOU and your life. Knowing the benefit you wish to achieve gives your journaling a purpose. When you have a purpose you can be creative with the types of journals you use to experience the benefits of journaling in your life.

JOURNALING FROM A PLACE OF HURT

It can be easy and fun to begin journaling and documenting the best of things in your life, but if you're journaling from a place of hurt it can be hard to get started. There are many times when journaling doesn't not come easy due to traumatic life events, a loss, a hurtful past, or other life challenges that prevent you from writing. Truth is, it is during these times when you can express your innermost thoughts to help you better cope with life, overcome life challenges, discover hope, and see life with a new perspective.

Challenge yourself to overcome the resistance of journaling and give it a try. As with everything in life, journaling will get easier for you with time. Use the "types of journals" list to help you identify a journal for your own individual needs. Connect with Let's Write Life on Facebook and YouTube to be inspired by the stories of others.

The success with making journaling a part of your life comes when you discover you can live and write your way through anything!

Yup, I still got it!!!

These are pictures of the front, back, and inside pages of my very first journal.

WATCH THE VIDEO

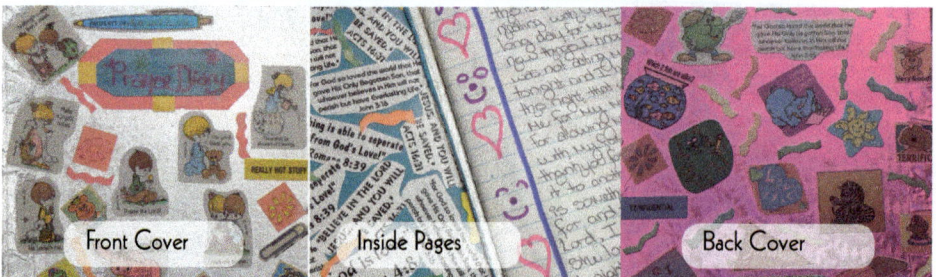

Front Cover

Inside Pages

Back Cover

What's the Point?
Give Your Journaling A Purpose.

JOURNALING PROMPT:

What goals, dreams, and aspirations do I want to accomplish over the next six months?

In the three boxes below, list your Top 3 goals and why these goals are most important to you. What do you want to overcome, gain clarity on, or move forward with in your life right now? When you have determined your goals, you can begin journaling in a way to achieve them!

Use the "Benefits of Journaling" and "Types of Journals" list on the following pages to help you experience the full benefits of journaling with your words leading the way.

MY TOP 3 GOALS AND THEIR IMPORTANCE IN MY LIFE:

1.

2.

3.

It's time to move forward! Let's Write Life!

Empower Your Greatness: Benefits of Journaling

With journaling, the benefits are numerous. From this list below, think about what would inspire you to begin journaling. Whatever you chose, set a goal to achieve it through journaling. **Circle or highlight the topics that stand out to you.**

RELIEVE STRESS:

- Allows you to escape the chaos of life
- Redirects your attention, thoughts, and emotions
- Allows space for your mind to be at ease
- Exhales all tense emotions
- Expresses your honest feelings without filters
- Allows you to think beyond your current challenges
- Helps you to understand your frustrations
- Gives peace of mind and reduces anxiety
- Allows focus, freedom, and inner peace
- Loosens emotional tension
- Brings out thoughts on paper to leave and return with clarity
- Channels feelings into words
- Enhances the enjoyment of personal hobbies or interest
- Organizes your thought process naturally
- Improves physical health and mental well-being
- Brings you to a calm state of mind

ACHIEVE YOUR POTENTIAL:

- Reveals what's meaningful to you
- Reveals the purpose inside of you
- Restores wholeness
- Prioritizes what is important
- Expresses who you truly desire to be
- Builds confidence in your abilities
- Maps out your thought process towards achieving goals
- Deepens your spirituality, insights, and intuition
- Tracks your progress

- Resolves your worries
- Helps to aid bad habits
- Helps to prepare for challenges ahead
- Gives insight of life lessons to be learned from past experiences

INCREASE SELF-AWARENESS:

- Reveals self-worth and deepens self-love
- Improves self-esteem
- Quiets your inner critic
- Keeps life in perspective
- Helps you observe how things make you feel
- Reveals what you know about yourself
- Helps you feel better about yourself
- Gives insight to your own wisdom
- Clarifies why you feel and behave certain ways
- Prevents self-sabotage
- Allow you to perceive the factors affecting your mood and ability to change them
- Shows the way you think, learn, and explore creativity
- Increases intuition and discernment
- Increases your insight into a situation
- Expresses what has remained unsaid
- Removes the mask that hides your true feelings and your true self

HEAL AND RESTORE:

- Creates the space to heal and let go of the past
- Releases true feelings from your heart
- Breaks down mental walls and barriers
- Provides an outlet to freely express your hurt and pain

- Confronts automatic negative thoughts
- Gives insight to your thought process and recurring patterns
- Helps to cope with a loss and eases the grieving process
- Brings healing to your emotional needs
- Records your thoughts as you welcome new beginnings
- Recalls memories to better understand their impact on your life
- Connects the dots to the root of current or past issues
- Helps manage behavior and inner and outer conflicts
- Eases vulnerability to share your life with others honestly and without fear and judgment
- Views your thoughts from a different perspective
- Lets your emotions guide your writing
- Addresses specific issues
- Releases what you need to say to yourself or someone else
- Releases emotions you once held back due to fear or embarrassment
- Eases the conversation and guides your participation during therapy
- Revisits your past with the adult wisdom you have now
- Helps overcome depression
- Prevents suicide and loneliness
- An outlet when no one else is there
- Brings comfort to past hurt
- Empowers your ability to overcome challenges
- Strengthens your confidence
- Helps let go or restores hurtful relationships
- Allows you to discover happiness and joy

POSITIVELY IMPROVE YOUR THINKING:

- Connects the dots of internal ideas to clear planning of goals
- Brings forth your desires and your truth to outweigh negative thoughts
- Improves writing and communication skills
- Increases productivity in your life
- Breaks large visions into attainable steps

- Sorts short-term and long-term goals
- Reveals personal areas of strengths and weakness
- Reveals what feels right in decision making

PRESERVE THE MEMORIES OF YOUR LIFE:

- Captures what matters to you
- Strengthens memories of events
- Leaves a legacy
- Helps to record the past with a positive outlook
- Brings out the things that give you joy
- Renews family bonds
- Reminds yourself of your accomplishments
- Helps you re-experience your past in a creative way
- Tells the many stages of you life in your own words
- Preserves the past memories of loved ones

EXPLORE SELF-EXPRESSION:

- You can write, draw, use audio, or type
- Write at your own pace, no editing, no filters required
- Can write your way through anything
- It can be whatever you need it to be whenever you need it
- There are no limits or boundaries
- Guides you to new levels of creativity
- Non-judgmental and private
- A source of empowerment

UNLOCK YOUR PURPOSE AND PASSION:

- Draws excitement to your ideas
- Explores curiosity and imagination
- Awakens great spiritual revelations
- Communes with your inner voice
- Inspires ideas that may evolve to future goals
- Helps you discover present everyday joy
- Explores dreams and visions
- Connects the dots to make your dreams a reality

A Journaling Lifestyle: Types of Journals

A journal is more than written words. Journals serve many purposes. On this list, I share several types of journals along with entry ideas you can apply to improve your life.

When most people think of journaling, they think of keeping a diary or just writing what's on their mind. This list of journals will certainly help you explore and expand everything you knew about journaling.

For each of these ideas you can create a brand new journal for each topic **OR** you can combine some of them into one journal. Choose whatever way works best for you.

If you're using more than one journal, it's important to remember you don't need to write in all of them every day.

"THE BEST OF ME" Journal —This journal is to record all the people, experiences, and everything in your life that brings out the best of you in a positive way that empowers you to move forward. With this journal, you can look inwardly at yourself in a way that will raise your self awareness and discover present joy in your life. Each page can be a source of empowerment holding all the ideas, plans, and goals you have for your life right now and your future. Let it be your space that encourages you when you are facing challenging times and uplift you when you need to reflect. Each page is a new opportunity to capture life in ways that truly bring out The Best of You!

Share your Best of Me journey with hashtag #mybestofme on Instagram. Connect with Let's Write Life on YouTube and Instagram for tips to fill your Best of Me Journal.

Video Link: Goo.gl/1o2TAl

Scan To Watch Videos →

Daily or Reflective Journal – This type of journal is for daily use to express whatever is on your mind, capture memories, reflect, vent, or record the day with no rules, without limits, and no judgment. Daily journals are whatever you need them to be; It's your life day by day or overtime. This is a great journal to help relieve your mind of stress during life's challenges and record daily successes in a private and personal way.

Idea Journal – Inspiration for a new idea can hit at any moment and this type of journal makes it easy to record ideas as they occur throughout the day. I found this type of journal extremely helpful when I needed to be creative or had an idea for a goal I wanted to achieve. This journal helps to capture all your ideas in one place and in writing for you to explore them with clarity.

Prayer and Meditation Journal – Prayer journals are great to write about your spiritual walk with God, to capture and communicate your prayers in writing, and to record revelation of answers to things you have prayed for. This journal encourages communication with God and enhances meditation.

Use this journal to organize devotional notes that will help you reflect on a passage you have heard and want to mediate on.

Quotes & Joy Journal

Quotes & Joy Journal – This journal is a stress buster and confidence booster to guide positive thoughts. In this journal you can write quotes about anything that make you smile, feel great, and make you laugh. Jot down jokes, songs, movies that lift you up and make you feel good, add quotes, scriptures, and funny pictures or stories that bring you joy. This is a journal for laughter that will turn any 🙁 into a 🙂 when you need to be encouraged to laugh your stress away. In the **RELAX. LIVE. CREATE.** journaling activities section, I share my personal story and techniques for journaling to relax.

Possibilities Journal – This journal is to record your dreams, visions, and aspirations you desire for your life that do not currently exist. Journaling about your dreams helps you to visualize and make clear your thoughts of what a better life truly looks like to you. This type of journal is used similarly to how many people use vision boards. You can include journal entries, create picture collages, phrases, words art, or other items that represent hopes of the life you desire to have.

Letter Journal – Letter writing is a past-time tradition that I would love to see continued in meaningful ways! In the meantime, this particular journal lets the essence of history be preserved by capturing your handwritten letters or cards you have written to people you care for. This journal can also be used to hold copies of letters you have received. Holding on to meaningful letters recalls memories and allows you to reflect on words of encouragement, love, or personal notes that have been written to you or that you've shared with others.

Gratitude Journal – In this journal you can express everything in your life that you are grateful of. This journal encourages positive thinking and releases negative thoughts, by helping you focus your attention on the good things that outweigh the bad. You may write something once a day in a list form or a full journal entry. Journaling in this way increases your happiness and overall well-being as you consciously send those negatively thoughts running because of your appreciation in the simplest aspects of life all around you.

Family Journal – This journal is to capture the memories of your family and the relationships you share with them. This journal can hold entries shared by family members or to tell the story of your family from your perspective. Family journals are a great way to capture notes of love or memorabilia during significant events that bring families together and to have printed as keepsakes.

Memory Journal – Apart from journaling to express daily thoughts and ideas, this journal focuses attention to specific moments of your life that you wish to explore and capture the memories of more in depth. These moments are past memories such as what you loved most about your childhood, things you use to do with your parents or siblings, what learning how to drive was like, the moment when you realized you had grown up, or any moment you wish to relive. This is also a great journal to record the memories of your children or someone else that has impacted your life. This journal is where you can explore lasting memories of your life.

5-Year Journal – This is an awesome journal to catch a glimpse of your life over five years as you record one line a day. This type of journal typically has a pre-made layout to show today's date and within that page there are sets of lines for you to capture your thoughts for each year. This type of journal is a great way to reflect and see the progression of your life over the years. Pre-made 5-Year Journals can be found on-line or in bookstores.

Collectible or Hobby Journal – In this journal you can keep track of all the details relating to hobbies and unique souvenirs that you collect. This journal helps you remember the significant details of your special interest, where they came from, and your memories of them. You can keep track of souvenirs and other memorabilia that you would want to maintain in this journal with pocket folders, envelopes, and photo sleeves for safekeeping's.

Goal Tracking Journal – This is a journal to direct all your attention towards strategies and ideas for reaching goals. This is a great way to help you focus on short-term or long-term goals you'd like to accomplish. In this journal set clear goals for yourself in writing, draw goal charts, or simply outline next steps you plan to take. As you experience success or setbacks, you can record your progress, new ideas, and keep notes for future planning and reflection.

Writer's Journal – There are those who love to journal and there are those who love to write! As writing is the forefront of journaling, what I mean here is a journal specifically for helping authors or aspiring writers to guide their writing process. This journal is great to capture ideas for publishing, taking down inspiration for storylines, or creating new characters for a book. This journal helps bring together all your creative thoughts for well-written works.

Dream Journal – For many of us, dreams may or may nor come to often. When you can remember your dreams, you can write them down for deeper reflection and insight to explore them. This journal may help you notice a pattern of occurrences or a new understanding of something that has been on your mind. Recording your dreams can be a great inspiration that enhances creativity in other areas of your life. I certainly think some of my dreams can make for a great book or one funny movie!

Book or Movie Journal – Do you remember reading a book that just left a great lasting impression with you? How about watching a movie that left you thinking? In this journal you can record names, titles, and reviews of your favorite books and movies you've enjoyed or have been recommended to you. For the best of both worlds, notes kept in this journal make great conversations starters at book clubs and discussions around movies based on books.

Diet and Exercise Journal – In this journal you can keep a record of your daily regimens, workout routines, and target dates for weight loss or health and wellness check –in's. This is an easy way to keep track of your strengths and weakness towards attaining your goals. This journal can be used to help you see what strategies, work out environments, and fitness trainings work best for your specific needs.

Art Journal – Art journals, also known as visual journals, are all about self-expression through a combination of art and text. With these journals you can express feelings in the most beautiful visual forms or just a frantic scribble to relieve stress. I love using drawing pads for visual journaling so that I can prop them on my desk or side table to display what I've drawn or written. Seeing the art openly brings inspiration to me throughout the day.

You can check out some of my Art Journaling on-line.

Blog Link: Letswritelife.com/category/art-journaling/

Health Journal — If you need to keep track of your physical well-being or health concerns, this journal can help guide conversations with you doctor or other healthcare professionals to inform them about what is happening with your body. You can also use this journal to note feedback during appointments, recommendations by your doctor, and write down any questions you have. This is a great journal to track symptoms during pregnancy or battling any illness.

Hair Journal — For anyone transitioning from one hair type to another, or enduring the fight over cancer, this is a great way to record your journey. In this journal document hair tips, useful resources, and successful hair products you've used along the way. This is also a nice way to capture pictures of photos of your changing hair lengths and styles. If you make your own hair remedies or products, record what you used and the outcomes. This can also be a great way to record your personal experience with how your hair may have changed your identity, how others have reacted to your new look, and how you feel about the various reactions you've received from others.

Legacy Journal — This journal is to honor the life of loved ones through your memories of them. You can use this to express the things you've wanted to say before they passed or to capture memorabilia from their life. This is also a great way to jot down ideas for how you would like to honor a loved one in the way you live your life now. You may record places you've traveled or connected with to support on behalf of your loved one. You may even write about how your loved one contributed to your life and shaped who you are today.

Event Journal or Diary — When you wish to document the details and experiences of specific events, these types of journals help you preserve your facts and insights. Theses journals are also known as diaries. Famous and biblical icons from our history have been known to keep these types of journals. Their journals are now resources that give us insight and personal accounts of their life during historical events. Who knows? If you live to witness a major historical event and record your thoughts, your journal could be published for the world to see and learn from.

Recipe Journal — Are you a foodie (a person with a high interest in all things food related) or aspire to be? This journal is a great way to explore your experience in the kitchen, keep track of recipes, and record the outcomes of your dishes. In this journal you can also record recipes that have been shared with you, so you know whom to thank for a great meal! Makes notes of the different variations you have tried with the dish and how people enjoyed it. This journal could be a great heirloom of family recipes to be preserved and passed down.

Gardening Journal — Do you have a green thumb? This journal is to keep track of your experiences in your yard or garden. This is a great way to keep notes about best practices year to year and what you would like to try in upcoming seasons. If you are indoor gardening for year round healthy eating purposes at home, keep notes of the types of fresh herbs or produce you are growing for their nutritional value, seasonal food ideas, lengths of harvest times, and preservation. In this journal you can list stores and on-line resources that have helped you along the way.

Finance Journal — This is a great way to outline budgeting goals and plans for yourself or your family's financial future. You may track your savings and how you plan to generate more income. Keep a record of resources and people you have connected with to help you achieve you financial goals, so you can connect with them when you're ready to move forward. This is also a great way to keep track of life events that have helped or hindered for financial endeavors, so you can better plan for the future.

Blog Journal — Do you just love blogging or have wanted to start? Keeping a blog journal will help you plan for blog topics, events, and content you wish to share with your audience. Track the topics that you have a special interest in and record how you can share this information with your blog followers. Ideas are always flowing and you may connect with some other great blogs that share your interest, so keeping track of your connections and great blogs you've learned about in the blogosphere will be very helpful on your blogging journey!

Nature Journal — For those of you who love to take long walks, jogs, or be outdoors, keeping a nature journal is great way to capture your outdoor experience as you observe nature. You can capture the essence of the weather, sounds, animals, and everything about the environment that stands out to you. What thoughts came to your mind as you walked? This is a great stress buster as it allows you to escape the chaos of life and immerse into a naturally calming environment.

Couples Journal — This is a helpful journal for couples to enrich their communication with each other, to share words of love and admiration, or to share what is on their heart that might be hard to say. This journal is also a great way for couples to make notes of goals they wish to achieve together, dreams for the future, and record past-time memories of their relationship.

As long as this list is, these are still just a few examples. Journaling can be whatever you need it to be, whenever you need it! Now you can explore all the many possibilities that journaling provides to enrich your life, your well-being, and what you know about yourself.

Looking for more journaling inspiration? See how others are using their journals on-line at Facebook.com/LetsWriteLife or at instagram.com/letswritelife.

Travel Journal — A travel journal is a great way to record your experiences while on a trip or to make notes for things you wish to explore while traveling. Some destinations may be a one-time or first-time travel experience such as traveling abroad, a mission's trip, or working internationally. Recording your experiences, people you've met, and iconic landmarks will help you to express what you were feeling in the moment of being immersed in a new environment or culture. Having this journal allows you to relive your experience through your writing, pictures, and souvenirs long after your trip and for many years to come in a way that you can share with friends and family.

Here is a blog post I wrote to share my personal experience with my first travel journal.

Blog Link: Letswritelife.com/a-travel-journal/

CREATE
THE STORY

RELAX. LIVE. CREATE.
LESSON THREE

WHAT WORDS CANNOT EXPRESS,
YOUR HEART SPEAKS.

Every time you take a moment out of your day to spend time using your Best of Me journal you are not only journaling, but also giving time to yourself and creating an empowering showcase of your life. Everything you create here allows you to express your innermost thoughts, clear your mind, relieve stress, and explore journaling in ways you can continuously incorporate into your life. Let these captured memories continue to bring out the best of you!

As you are creating your Best of Me journal, think long term about how this life journal fulfills a purpose in your life. How you fill it up will be a reflection of how you've experienced your life along the way, so make it meaningful. The saying goes, a picture is worth a thousand words. CREATE is all about Art Journaling and bringing a picture of a thousand words to life visually.

Art journaling is nothing more than journaling in a way in which you combine words and images to express life's experiences, feelings, and innermost thoughts. Art journaling became meaningful to me during times in my life when I needed clarity of my thoughts, needed to relax, and wanted to express myself in a way that I could let off frustration or just seemed like fun. Let me tell you, it has become so much more!

Have you ever felt like life is throwing so many things at you at once that you just have to stop? When I began Let's Write Life, I had no idea just how much my life would empower others through journaling. Getting the business started was a lot of work. There were times when I was moving full speed ahead with great outcomes, times when things were stressful, times full of joy because of the work I was doing, and sometimes I just felt overwhelmed by it all. In these moments I would pull out my art journals, which consisted of large drawing pads or blank pages in my notebook to visually express how I felt. I have used art journaling for relaxation, reaching goals, developing vision boards, and decision-making. Making thoughts visual connects the dots of confusion and enhances clarity. My art journals are anchors in my life that I continuously use to freely write quotes and draw words of affirmation, draw out thought webs to clarify my thoughts, and create vision boards to keep me motivated and keep things in perspective for me.

The benefits to visual journaling are unlimited! The same benefits of writing applies to art journaling. Different art journaling techniques can be used to achieve your individual goals. When was the last time you pulled out colored pencils, crayons, or markers and just sat down to color or draw something? Seemed so natural when we were young, why not now? In this season of your life I want to encourage you to give art journaling a try, even if you think you do not have an artistic bone in your body. The experience of art journaling and discovering your own self-expression may be the very thing that brings you much joy. Within this life journal, I have set aside wide page margins and blank journaling pages you can fill in with art journaling. Be creative and make these spaces your own.

WHERE FRIENDS MEET, THERE IS JOY.

Art Journaling can be enjoyed individually and within groups. Learn from others new art journaling techniques, watch on-line tutorials, sign up for journaling workshops or other creative art classes to deepen your artistic curiosity. My hope is that in filling up your life journal you will be empowered to explore journaling in a new way.

Here are 10 Art Journaling ideas to help you get started:

1. CREATE a Personal Manifesto page. This will be your "word art" of empowerment to invoke change, foster commitment in seeing the best of yourself, and to remember what really matters to you. A Manifesto is all word-based and consists of personal statements that declare your beliefs. Fill it with inspiration, positive affirmations, bible verses, quotes, words of wisdom, and goals you want to see every time you need to be encouraged and empowered to see the Best of YOU! Need some help getting started, search "Personal Manifestos" or "Personal Affirmations" on-line and read what others have written for inspiration.

2. Listen to an empowering message or music. The experience of art journaling can be very empowering if you make this a time to listen to a motivational message while you are drawing. Listening to an empowering message, playing music, or watching an art journaling tutorial while drawing out key words, quotes, and phrases that have inspired you while listening will leave you feeling so refreshed. Feel free to use on-line resources such as YouTube.com to listen to your favorite inspirational speakers, motivational podcasts, or your own favorite music list to make your art journaling time empowering. Believe me, when you're done you will feel like you can conquer the world!

3. Choose a song that is meaningful to you and create word art with the lyrics or chorus of the song. Choose the part that speaks to your heart at this time in your life. (See My Sample Image on Next Page)

4. Create a thought web for this question: "What would I like to achieve by the end of this year?" (See My Sample Image on Next Page)
How Thought Webs Work:
Within a circle you would write a leading thought, question, or goal that you would like to focus on. Once you have your leading thought, list out as many supporting thoughts, steps, or task you must complete to fulfill the purpose of your leading thought. For all supporting thoughts, connect them to the leading circle with lines. Thought webs are great for brainstorming ideas.

5. Create a thought web for this question: "What Is Your Life Purpose?" You may not know. Write or draw anything. Perhaps, answer this question with many questions. No Limits. No Judgment. This is to get you thinking and to spur curious thoughts about yourself and your life.

6. Art journaling can be so much more than ink on a page, so challenge yourself to be creative. Add paint colors, scrapbook embellishments, pictures, and drawings to bring each page to life.

7. Let's draw! Zentangle is a fun and easy way to draw in a way that is relaxing, increases focus and creativity. Try Zentangle Method by filling in the wide page margins of your journaling pages as shown on the left hand side of the first lined journaling page.

8. A Vision Board is a collage of pictures, images, and affirmations to visually communicate your dreams. Create a vision board of things you desire in your life this year.

9. Dedicate art journaling space to people you love. Write their names and bring thoughts you have of them to life through adding color to their name, draw out positive words that describe them, write out a prayer for them, well wishes you desire for them, and add pictures and quotes as desired to show your appreciation of them.

10. Create "In Loving Memory" pages for loved ones you've lost. Use this as a special place to honor the memories of their life.

Let's Write Life! Go on-line and search "Art Journaling" for new ideas you can incorporate into your journaling space. Pinterest is a great resource for ideas! Be creative and have fun! Journaling is all about taking the time to express what's on your mind, in writing and visually. The more you do, the more you'll discover the way journaling works best for you.

Art Journaling Samples

Word Art

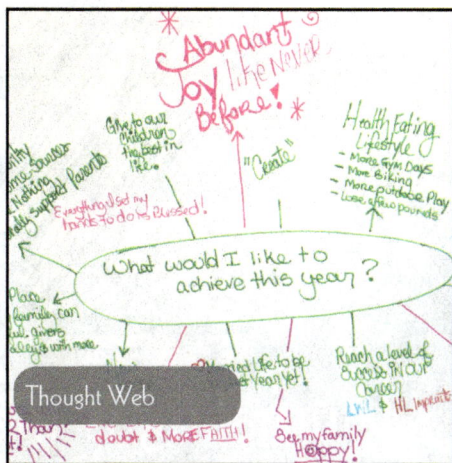

Thought Web

WHAT'S YOUR STORY?

How are you using "The Best of Me" Journal? What are you working on achieving in your life right now? Would you like to share your story to encourage someone else? How has journaling helped you? Share your journaling ideas and life stories on-line to inspire others. Your story can be the inspiration, the light in a dark place, or the motivation someone needs to hear that transforms their life in a meaningful way.

For years I suffered in silence with depression. During those times, it was extremely hard for me to reach out for help, which made me feel isolated and alone. Coming out of those dark times in my life it was the stories of others, my faith in God, and making a decision to turn my life around that changed everything for me. My healing began through my story.

Through our lives, we can all be apart of someone else's journey through the challenges we have been able to overcome.

SHARE YOUR STORY AND LIFT SOMEONE UP AT: **LETSWRITELIFE.COM/STORY.**
USE HASHTAG #MYBESTOFME ON INSTAGRAM AND FACEBOOK.

Journaling is the voice of your soul when your heart desires to express how you feel.

— Latonia

Journaling Pages

My Best Life Bucket List

If money and time were not an issue, what would I live my life doing without any regrets?
Push Yourself To List As Much As You Desire.

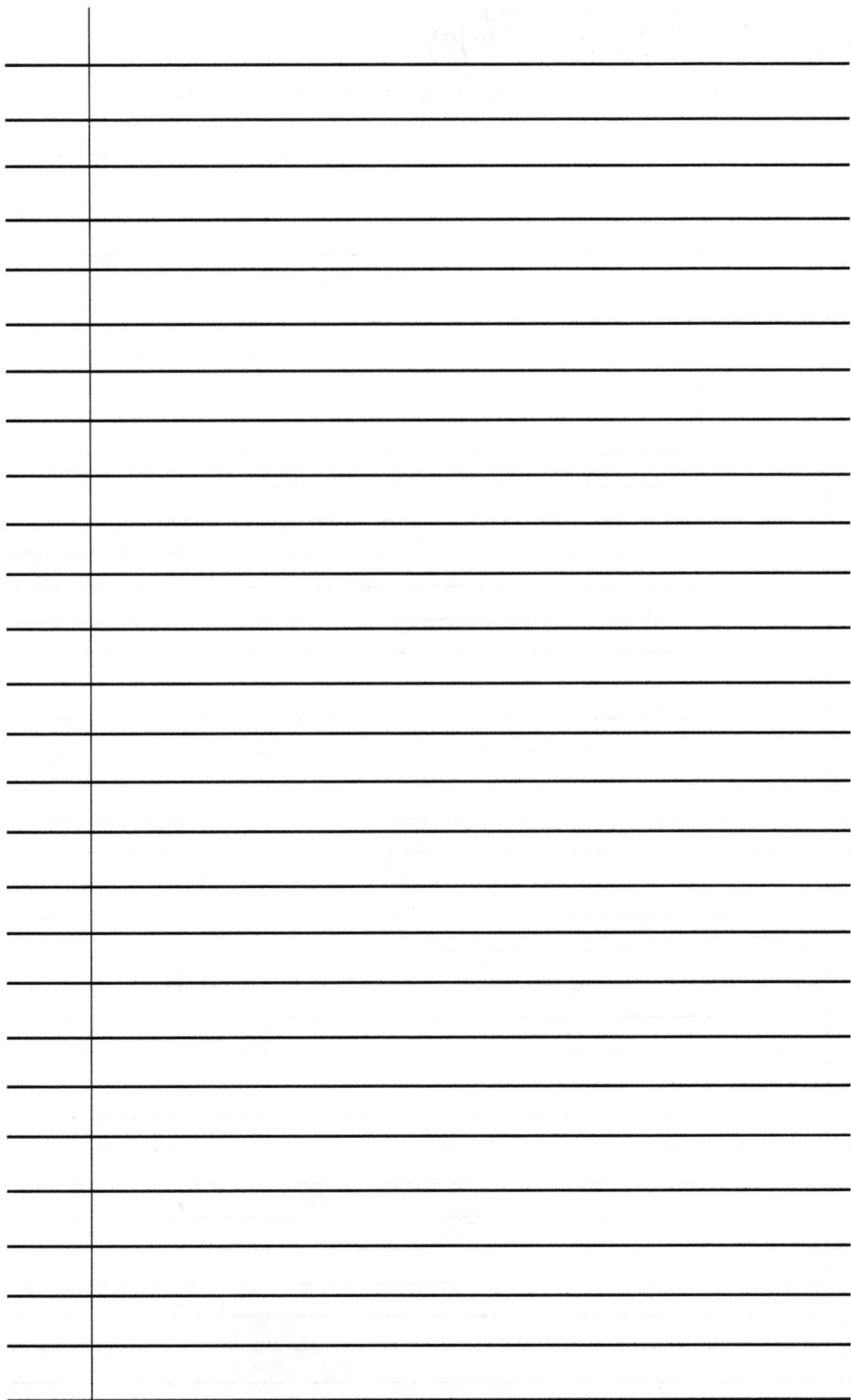

My Goals & Next Steps

What needs to be accomplished in order to keep moving forward toward your life goals?

- [ ] _____
- [ ] _____
- [ ] _____
- [ ] _____
- [ ] _____
- [ ] _____
- [ ] _____
- [ ] _____
- [ ] _____
- [ ] _____
- [ ] _____
- [ ] _____
- [ ] _____
- [ ] _____
- [ ] _____
- [ ] _____
- [ ] _____
- [ ] _____
- [ ] _____
- [ ] _____
- [ ] _____
- [ ] _____
- [ ] _____
- [ ] _____
- [ ] _____
- [ ] _____
- [ ] _____
- [ ] _____
- [ ] _____
- [ ] _____
- [ ] _____
- [ ] _____
- [ ] _____
- [ ] _____
- [ ] _____

My Goals & Next Steps

What needs to be accomplished in order to keep moving forward toward your life goals?

- [ ] _____
- [ ] _____
- [ ] _____
- [ ] _____
- [ ] _____
- [ ] _____
- [ ] _____
- [ ] _____
- [ ] _____
- [ ] _____
- [ ] _____
- [ ] _____
- [ ] _____
- [ ] _____
- [ ] _____
- [ ] _____
- [ ] _____
- [ ] _____
- [ ] _____
- [ ] _____
- [ ] _____
- [ ] _____
- [ ] _____
- [ ] _____
- [ ] _____
- [ ] _____
- [ ] _____
- [ ] _____
- [ ] _____
- [ ] _____
- [ ] _____
- [ ] _____
- [ ] _____
- [ ] _____
- [ ] _____
- [ ] _____

My Accomplishments & Milestones

Date   Accomplishments

My Accomplishments Continued...

Date   Accomplishments

_____   _____

_____   _____

_____   _____

_____   _____

_____   _____

_____   _____

_____   _____

_____   _____

_____   _____

_____   _____

_____   _____

_____   _____

_____   _____

_____   _____

_____   _____

_____   _____

_____   _____

_____   _____

_____   _____

_____   _____

_____   _____

_____   _____

Counting My Many Blessings

Date   Blessings

_____   _____

_____   _____

_____   _____

_____   _____

_____   _____

_____   _____

_____   _____

_____   _____

_____   _____

_____   _____

_____   _____

_____   _____

_____   _____

_____   _____

_____   _____

_____   _____

_____   _____

_____   _____

_____   _____

_____   _____

_____   _____

Counting My Many Blessings Continued...

Date   Blessings

_____   _____

_____   _____

_____   _____

_____   _____

_____   _____

_____   _____

_____   _____

_____   _____

_____   _____

_____   _____

_____   _____

_____   _____

_____   _____

_____   _____

_____   _____

_____   _____

_____   _____

_____   _____

_____   _____

_____   _____

_____   _____

_____   _____

_____   _____

_____   _____

Favorite Quotes

" _____
_____ "

" _____
_____ "

" _____
_____ "

" _____
_____ "

" _____
_____ "

" _____
_____ "

" _____
_____ "

" _____
_____ "

" _____
_____ "

" _____
_____ "

" _____
_____ "

" _____
_____ "

Favorite Quotes

"_____
_____"

"_____
_____"

"_____
_____"

"_____
_____"

"_____
_____"

"_____
_____"

"_____
_____"

"_____
_____"

"_____
_____"

"_____
_____"

"_____
_____"

"_____
_____"

JOURNEY OF CONTENTS
Journaling Prompts

There are many stories to be told that will fill the pages of this journal. On your journey, here are some themes to help guide you through. I encourage you to add something meaningful from your life that relates to each theme listed.

PEOPLE

This theme represents anyone that brings you joy. These are people that have impacted your life and mean everything to you. Think about relationships with a spouse, your children, someone you are dating, mentors, friends, family, and more. This theme also includes those who are in your life currently or have passed away. Honor your loved ones in this way by including why they are a meaningful part of your life story.

INSPIRATION

This theme is all about bringing together music, quotes, activities, scriptures, favorite movies, sermons, motivational messages, and anything that makes you feel motivated to persevere or take action. Make notes of them in your journal to easily be reminded of their essence when you need to redirect your focus.

ACCOMPLISHMENTS

What about your life are you grateful for? What are you proud of? For this theme, show what success means to you. This is where you can express self-love for your own success without judgment, comparing your life to someone else, and without feeling the need to meet the expectations of others. Becoming a parent, starting a business, achieving your degree, losing weight, ending or restoring relationships, beating cancer or other healthcare concerns, writing your first book or second book, getting published, buying a home, or getting that awaited promotion or new job are a few examples. Every step forward, big or small, is a meaningful part of you!

POSSIBILITIES

Curiosity and possibility can be explored through journaling. Write about dreams and goals you want to see come to life. Even if they seem impossible or crazy, let yourself express your hopes and dreams freely.

DESTINATIONS

Record all the places you have traveled or want to travel to that bring you joy. Think about places that may be more significant to you like revisiting your childhood hometown, birthplace, or my personal favorite...Disney. Other destinations might be where you experienced special occasions in your life.

PASTIME MEMORIES

This theme captures any memories you just have to get down on paper to remember for yourself, your loved ones, your kids, and even their kids. Think about what life was like for you growing up and capture the memories through your writing.

LETTERS TO MY YOUNGER ME

What are the things you would tell your younger self? What things mattered to you back then that now you wished you handled differently? Share the wisdom you have today with your younger self. These life lessons are a great way to reflect on what really matters.

BE CREATIVE AND HAVE FUN.

You are only limited by your imagination. Fill these pages with photos, use it for scrapbooking embellishments, art, and more! Showcase many events of your life or only capture one specific life event that really changed your life. Whatever your story, Let's Write Life!

COMMUNITY OF FRIENDS

I'd love to see what you've done with the place. Share your stories and post pictures from your Best of Me journal on IG using hashtag #mybestofme. See you there!

Watch Live Journaling Broadcast on: 　　　@letswritelife
Write to us at: www.letswritelife.com/story

Scan for Facebook

All Art
Over Here

I believed I could,
SO I DID ♡

LOVE
IS THE
CURE

Blank Space:
Within the blank page margins and
blank pages throughout the journal,
feel free to fill these spaces with
photos, QR codes, quotes, written
words, or art journaling.

The BEST
of ME

MY LIFE, EMPOWERED
MY STORY

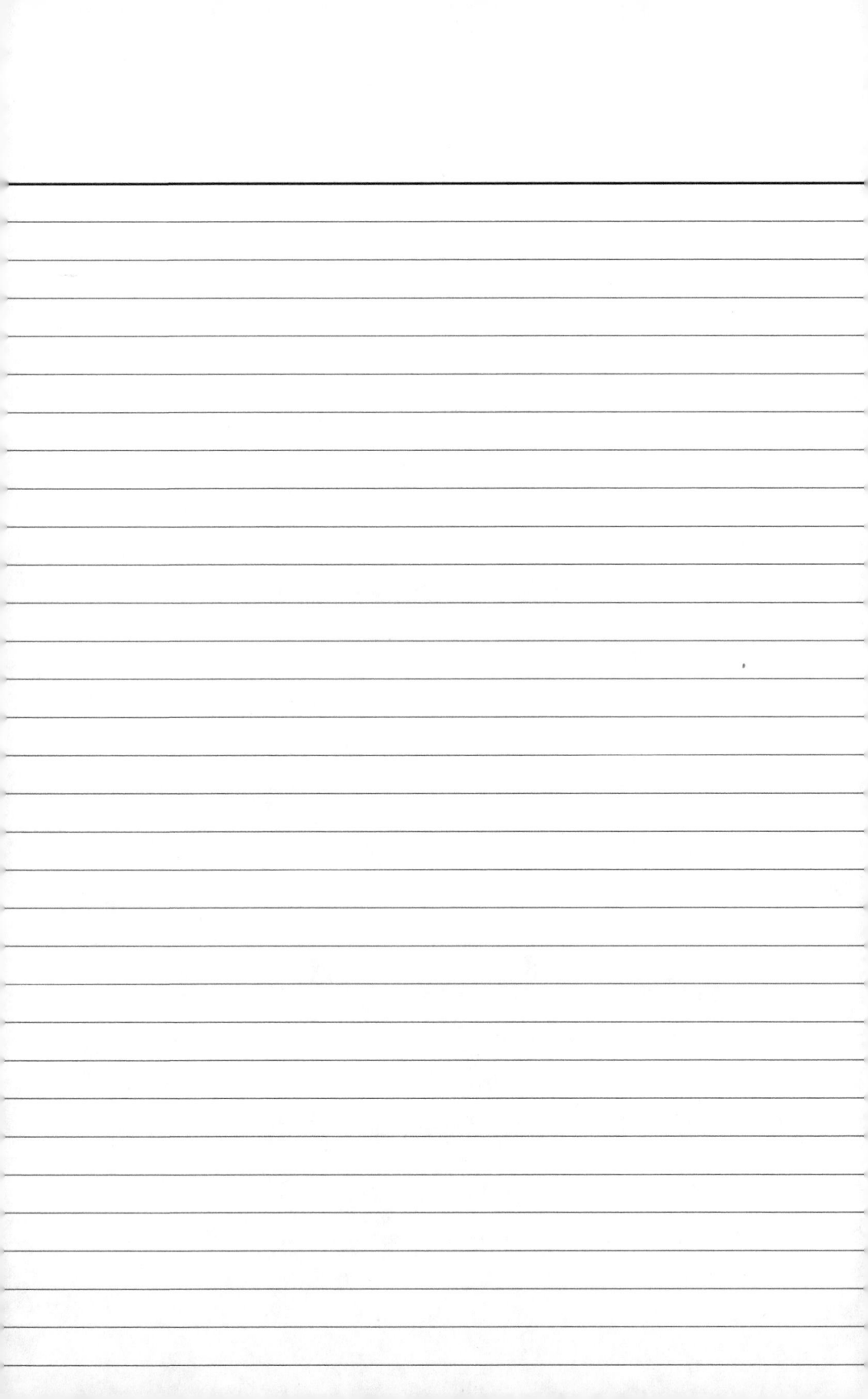

THE

BEST

OF

ME.

TODAY I CHOOSE HAPPINESS. THERE IS NO OTHER WAY.

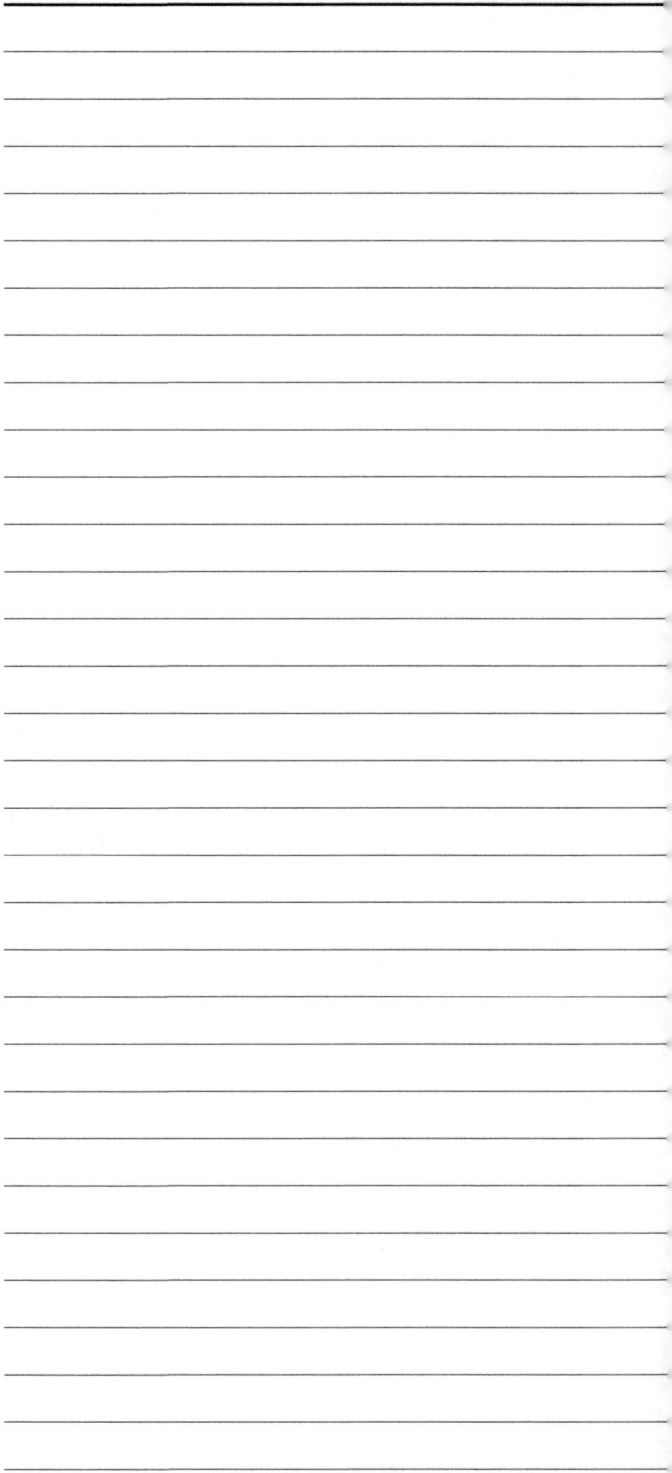

You are always stronger than you think. Believe in the hope inside of you.

LIFE
EVER
AFTER

EVEN IN THE
MIDST OF
DARKNESS
THERE CAN
BE LIGHT.

HAPPINESS
IS ALWAYS AN
INSIDE JOB.

TOUGH
TIMES DON'T
LAST. TOUGH
PEOPLE DO.

CHOOSE
JOY

DO
WHAT
REALLY
MATTERS

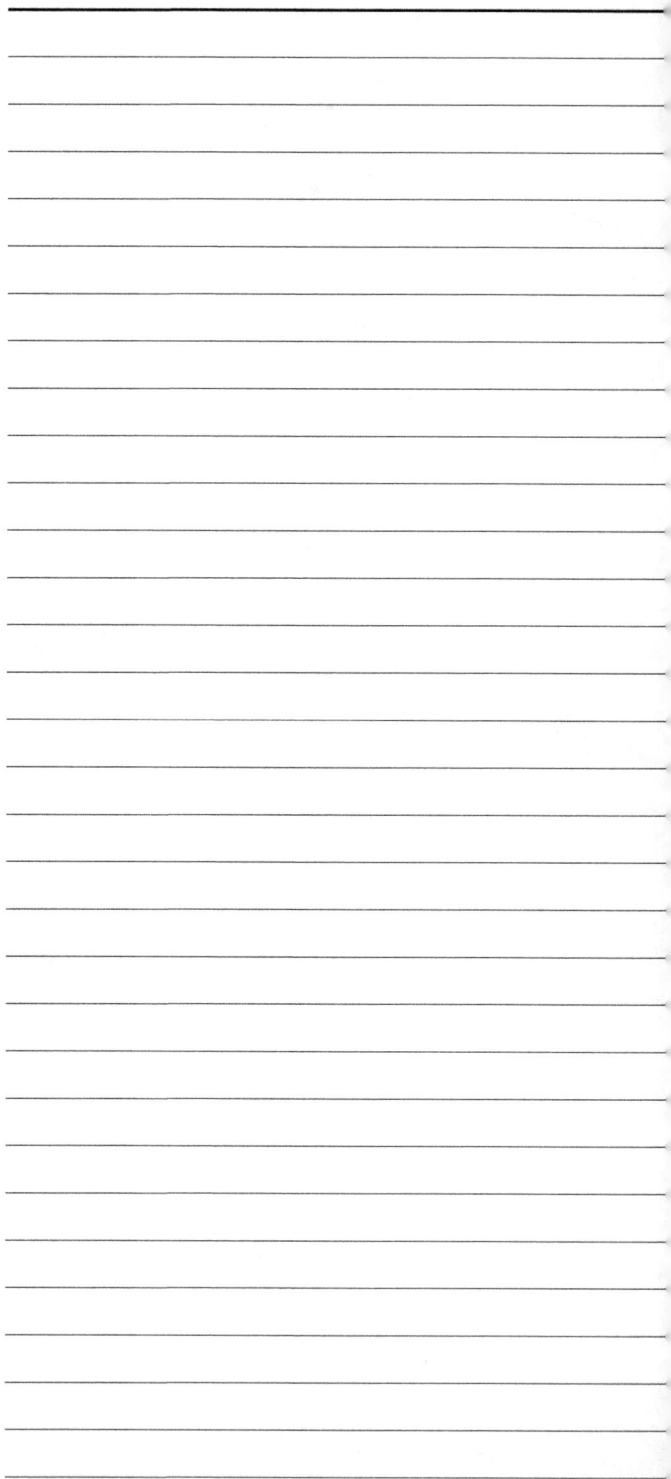

There were
times when...
I cried.
I laughed.
I smiled.
I Made It!

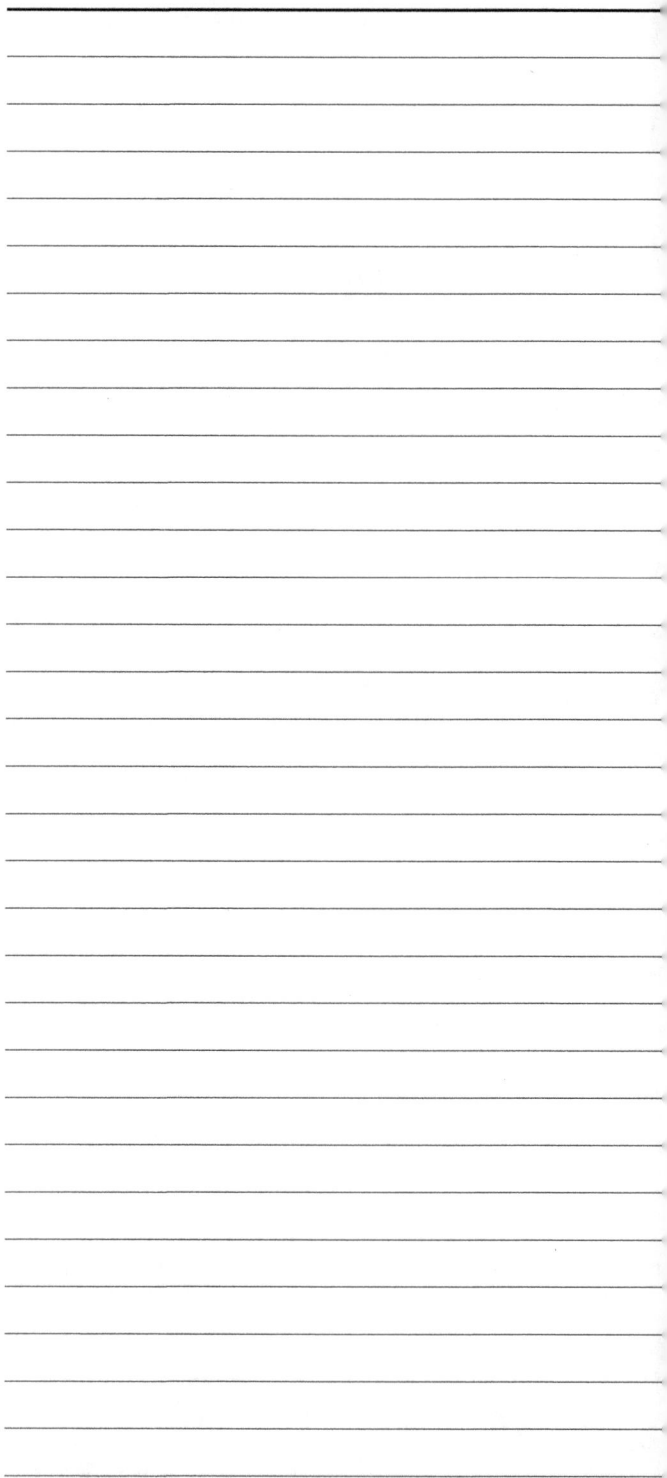

Live a
Life Worth
Writing About.

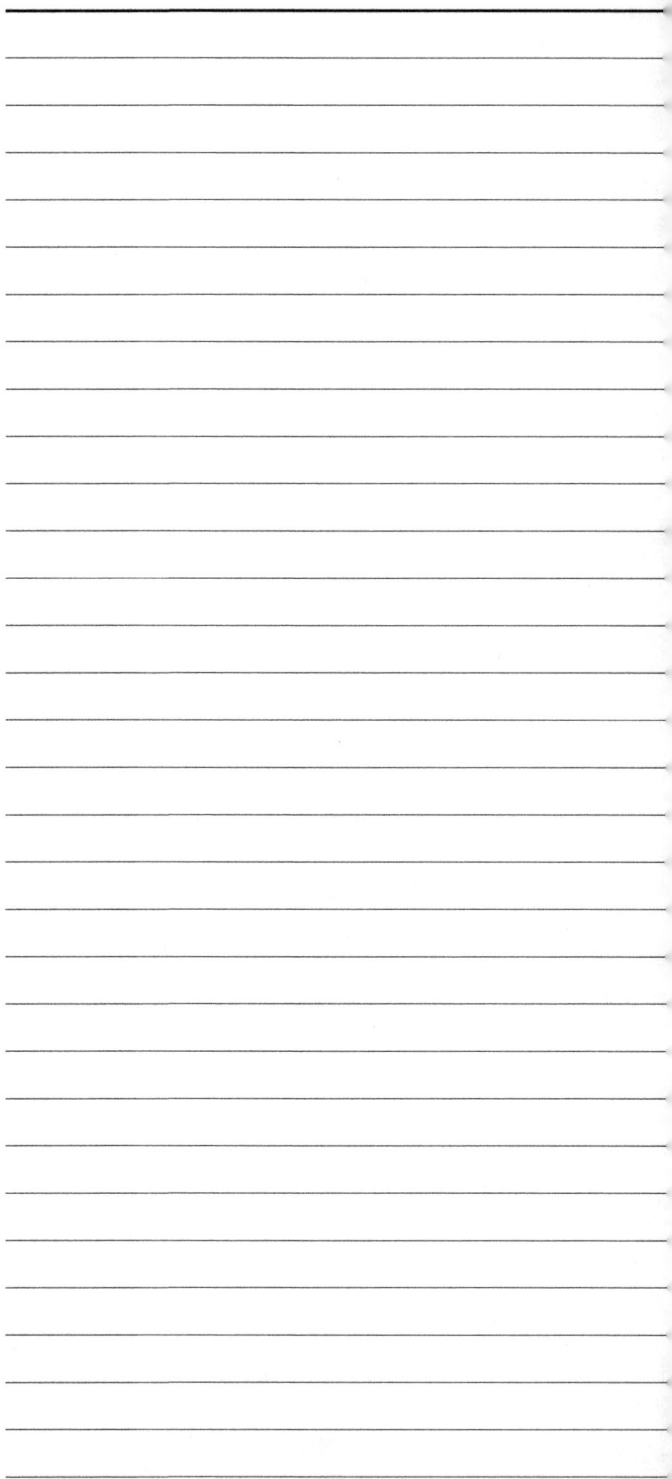

DON'T BE
AFRAID
TO DREAM
A LITTLE
BIGGER.

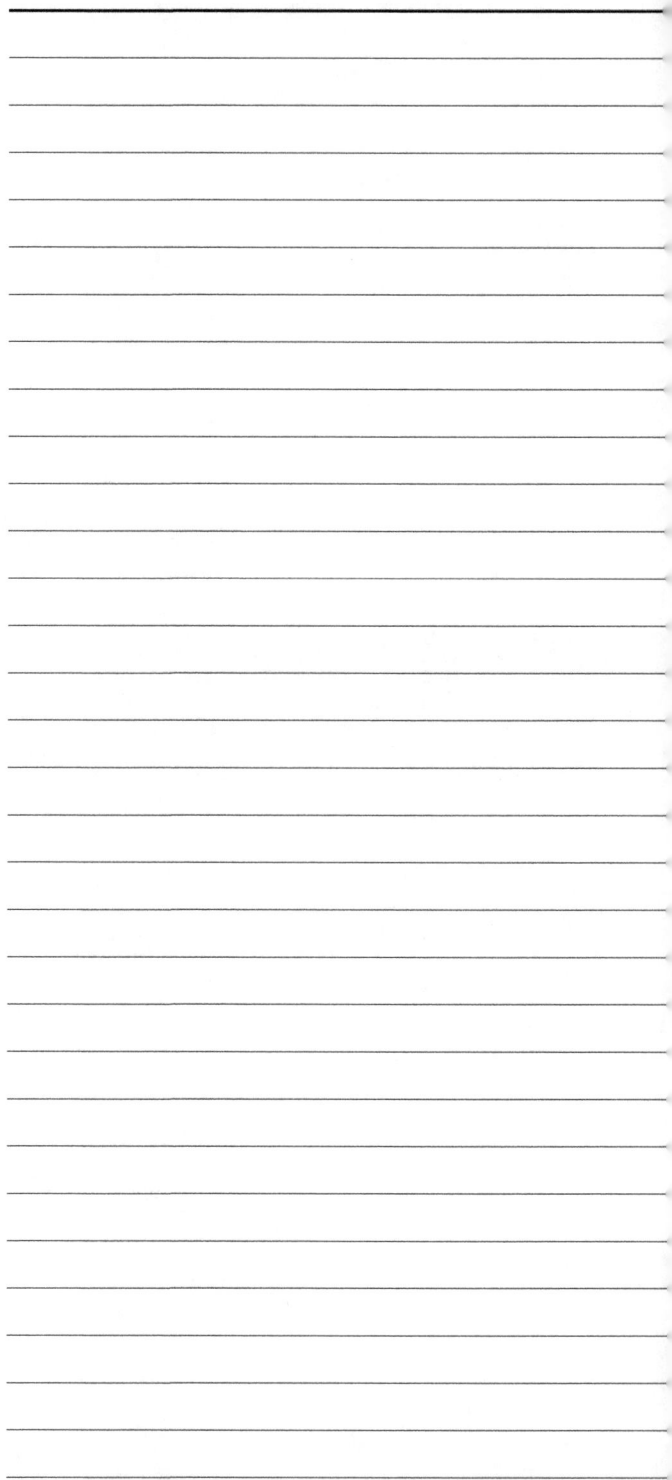

Live like
anything is
possible.

BREAK
EVERY
CHAIN

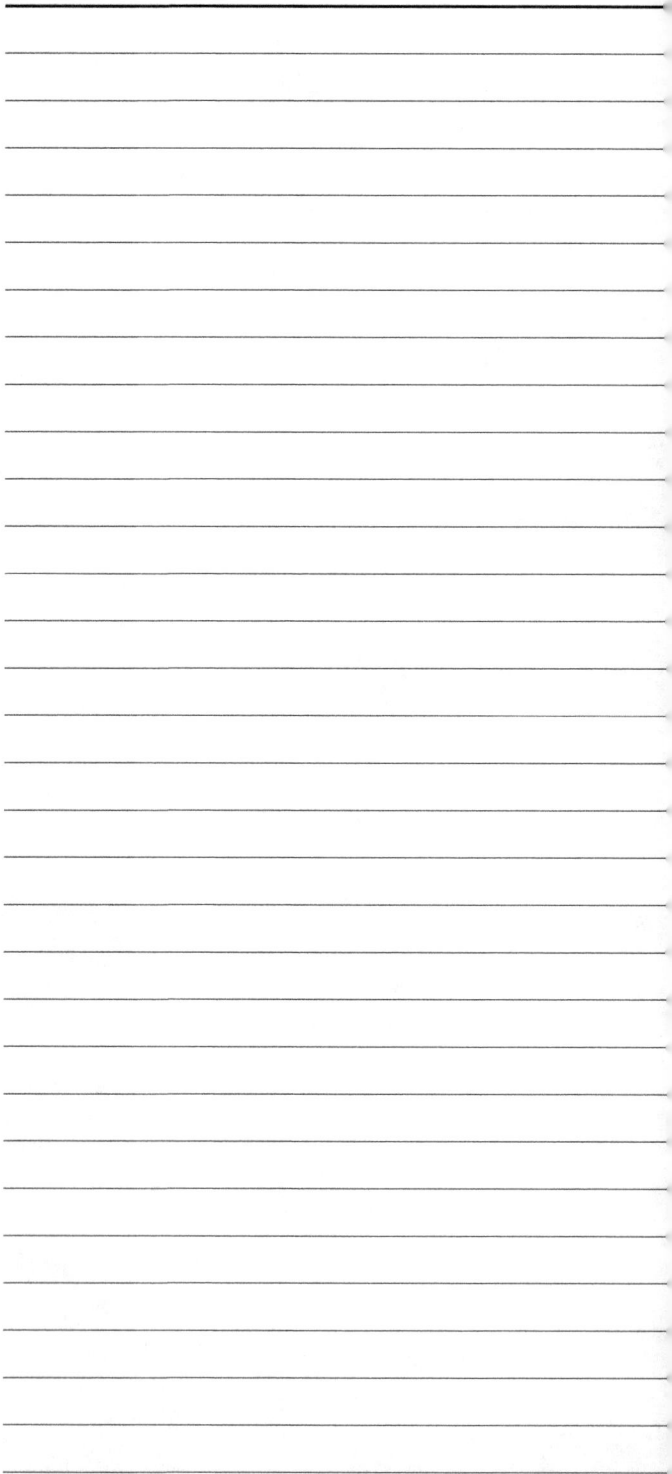

My best is yet to come.

I'M
LIVING
IN THE
MOMENT.

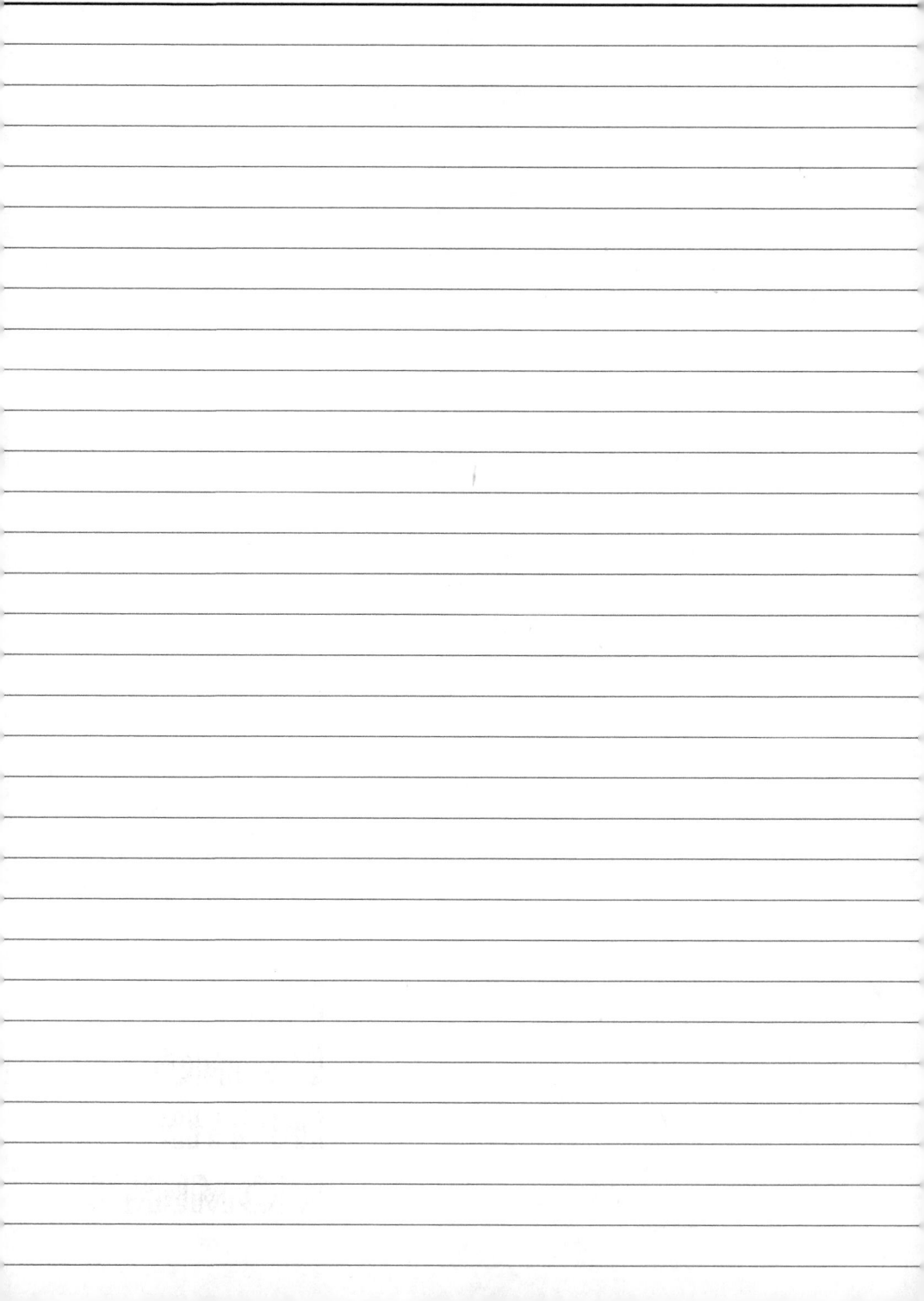

The more knowledge you have about who you are, the more understanding you'll have to be the person you desire to be.

When was the last time you did something fabulous for yourself? What did you do?

Write about the way you would most enjoy spending time alone.

WRITING PROMPT

WRITING PROMPT

Describe something you would like to do for yourself that no one else can do for you.

Self-love is the foundation on which we choose to love and accept ourselves for who we are. It is the start to building a fulfilling life from the inside out. Explore the meaning "self-love" and write your own definition of what it means to you.

WRITING PROMPT

WRITING PROMPT

In what ways have you overcome feeling discouraged by the opinions, comparisons, and negative thoughts of others?

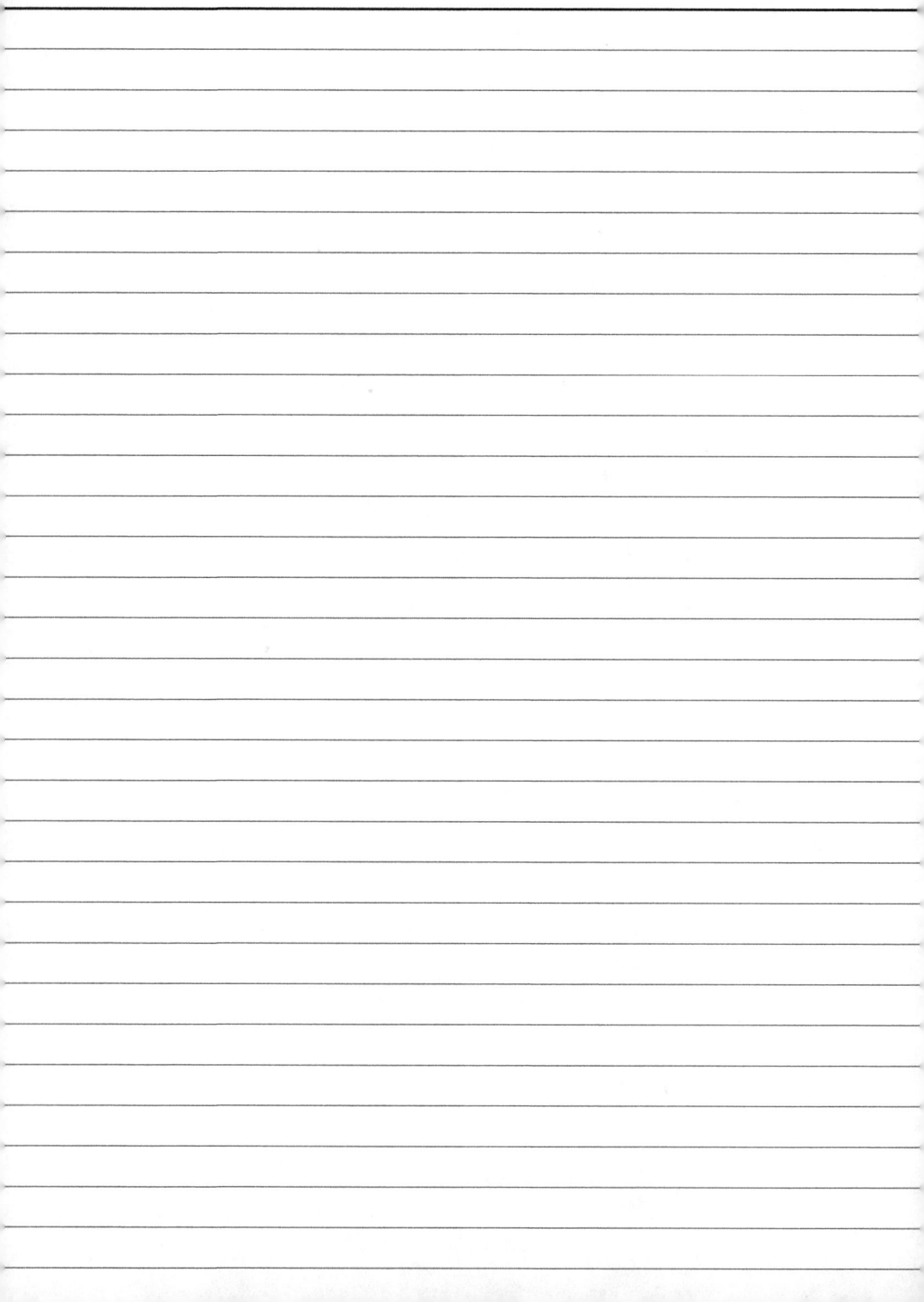

Faith, Family, Health, Love, and Joy are examples of core values. What are 5 core values that make you who you are? Why are these values important to you?

WRITING PROMPT

In what ways have you learned how to love who you are?

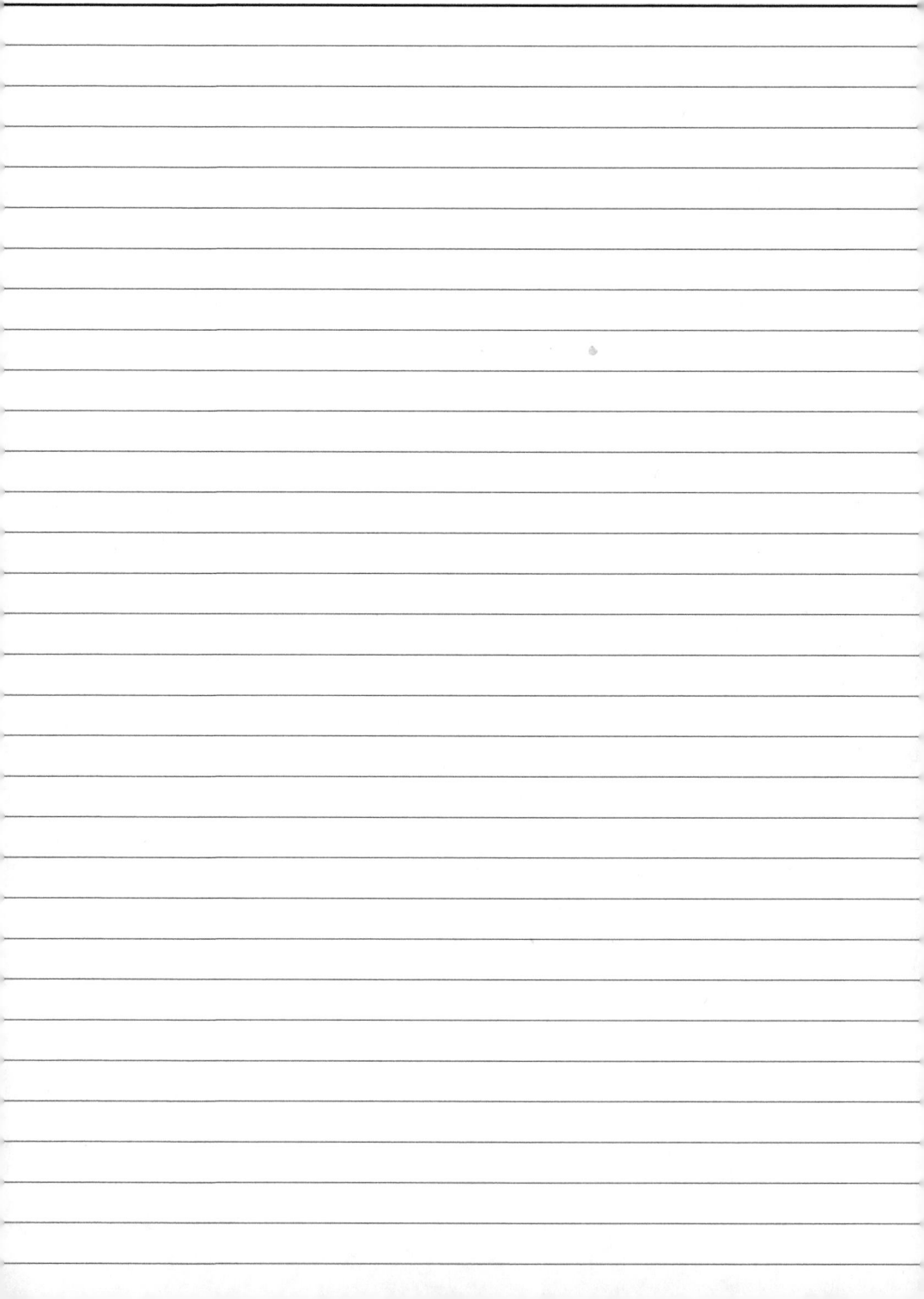

How has love changed in your
life over the years?

/ /

What situations make you feel like
you are not good enough?

WRITING PROMPT

Describe a time you were there for someone who really needed you to be there. You held someone's hand, gave them a call, wrote them a letter, told them you love them, or visited them just because you didn't want them to be alone. Who has been that person to you?

/ /

WRITING PROMPT

What are a few positive things people say about you that you do not believe about yourself?

/   /

You are not damaged. You are not worthless.
You are not dirty. You are beautiful and
deserve to be here. How does this statement
make you feel?

/   /

WRITING PROMPT

How do you overcome not feeling good enough?

/ /

WRITING PROMPT

What do you wish you could love more about yourself?

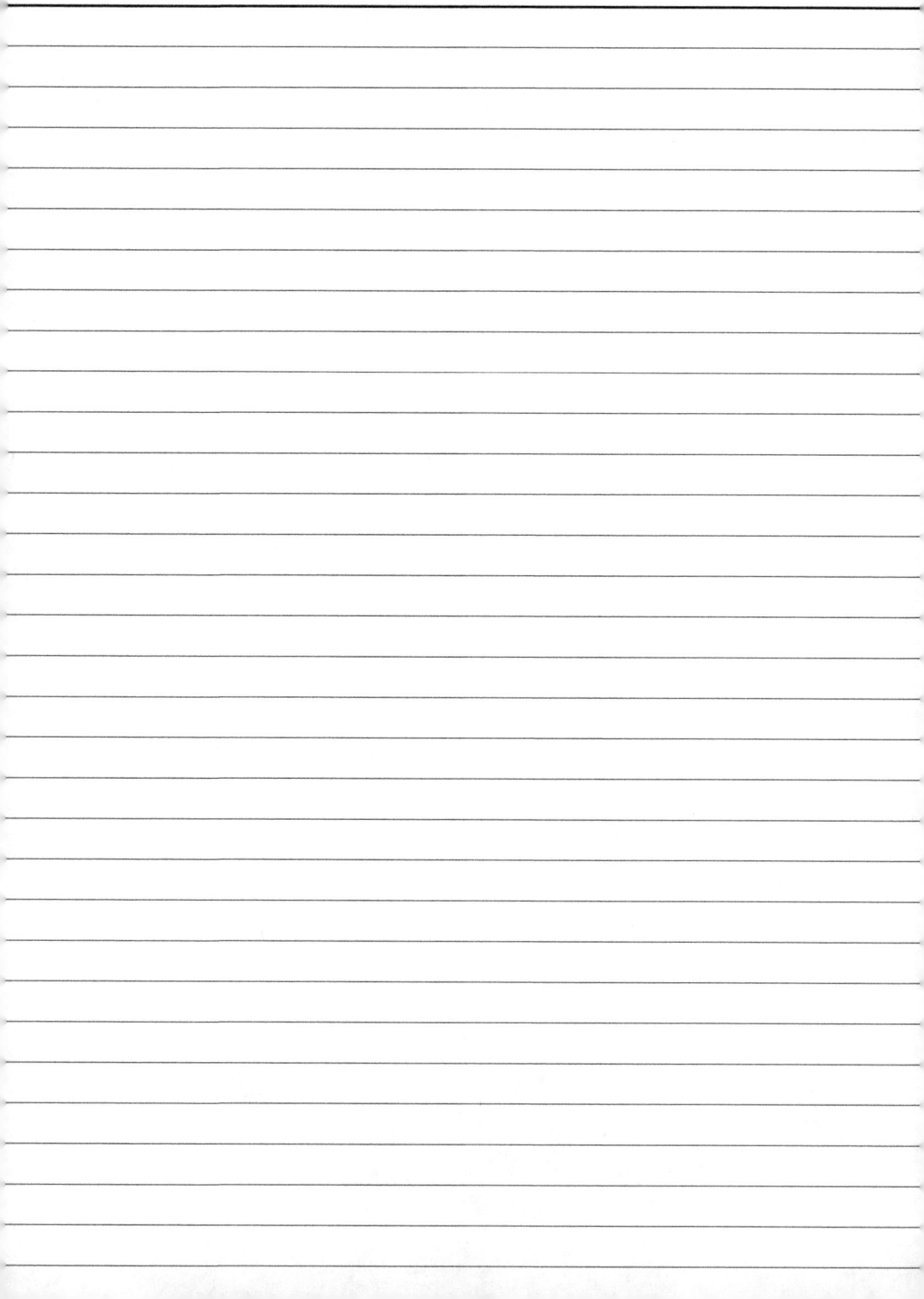

Your ability to change your life
starts by changing who you are
inside. What would you change?

/   /

Too positive to be doubtful, too optimistic to be fearful, too determined to be defeated.

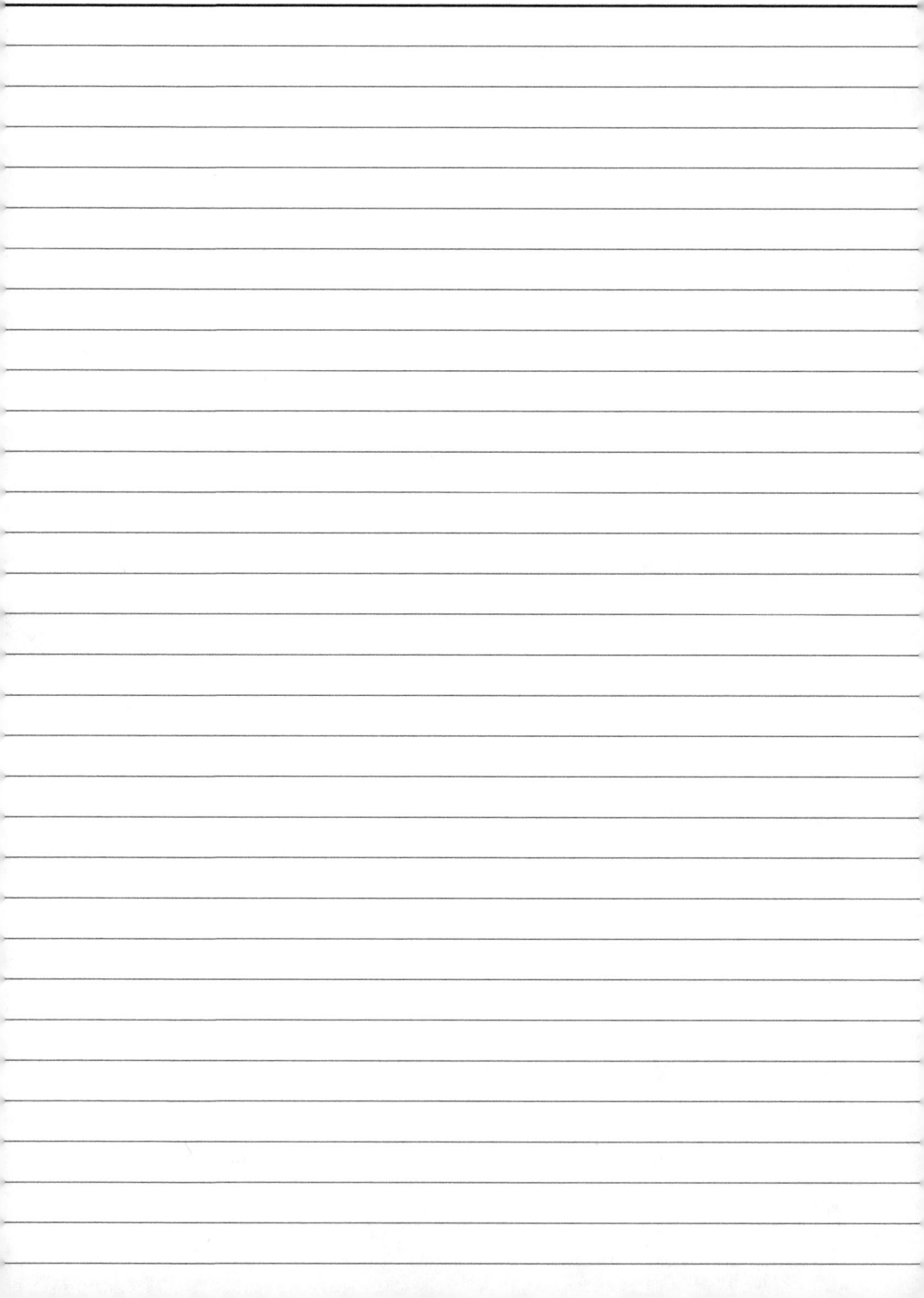

Strive for progress, not perfection.

You matter; no matter what you might think.

/   /

Achieve greatness. Aim for the top, land among the stars.

/   /

You can do this and so much more.

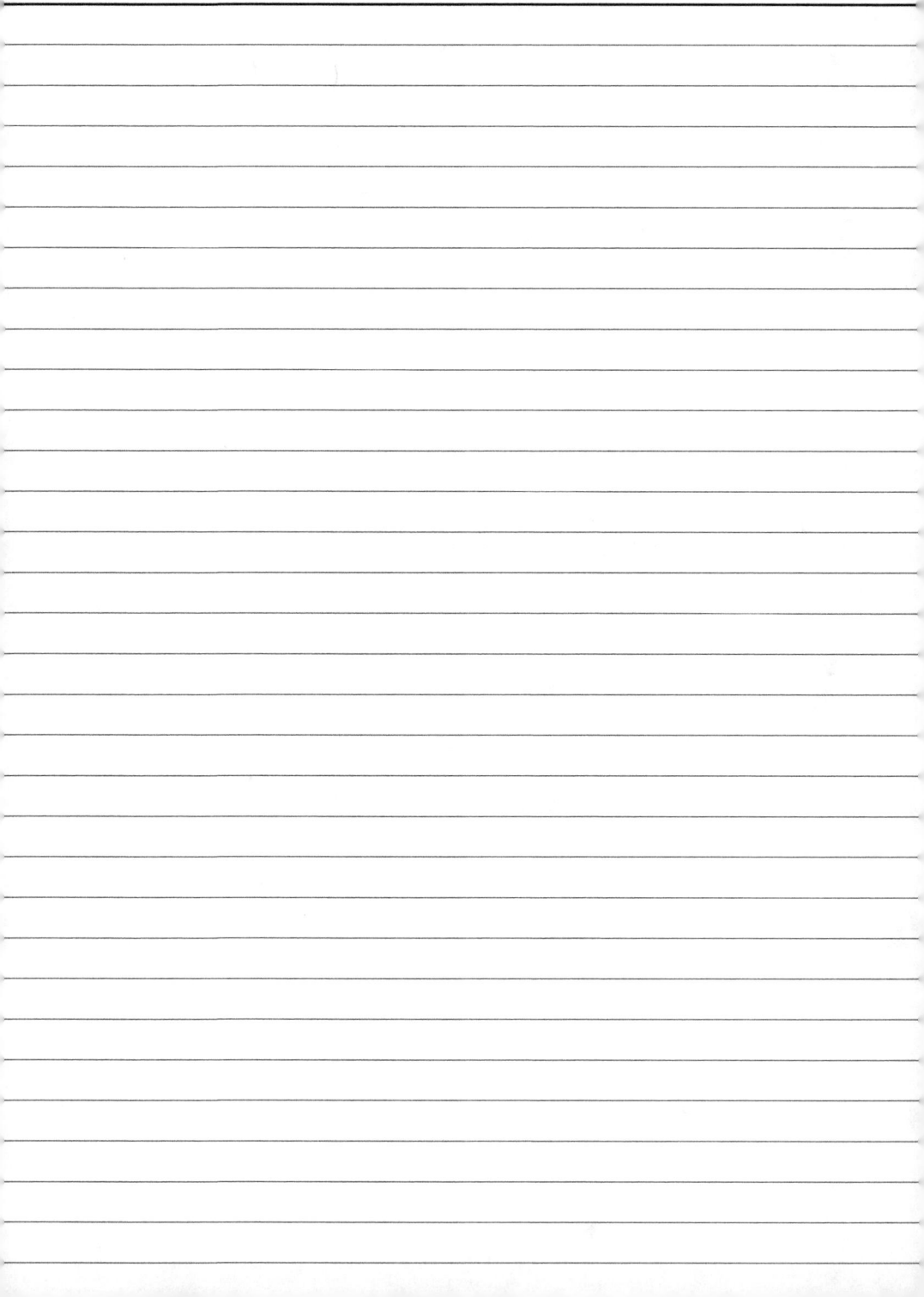

Don't stop until you're proud.

At the most pressing times when you are weak, that's when you are strong.

Live your life. Write it well. You are a success story.

/   /

The root of all joy is not found in things. It's found inside of you.

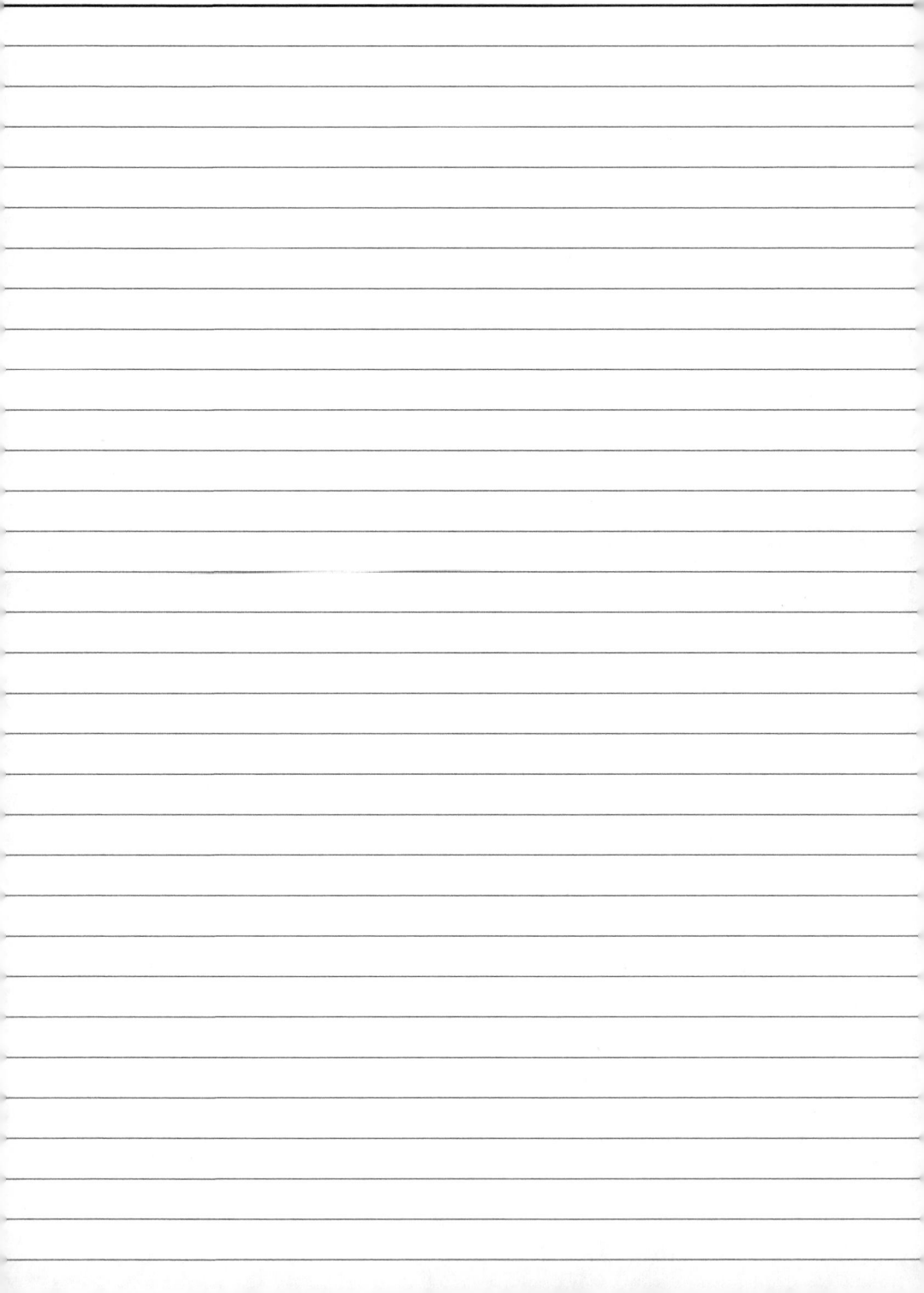

You don't have to be perfect,
you just have to start.

/   /

If it doesn't line up with your goals, don't let
it stand in the way of your purpose.

/   /

*Your only focus is to keep
your light lit.*

WRITING PROMPT

I love myself because I am _____.

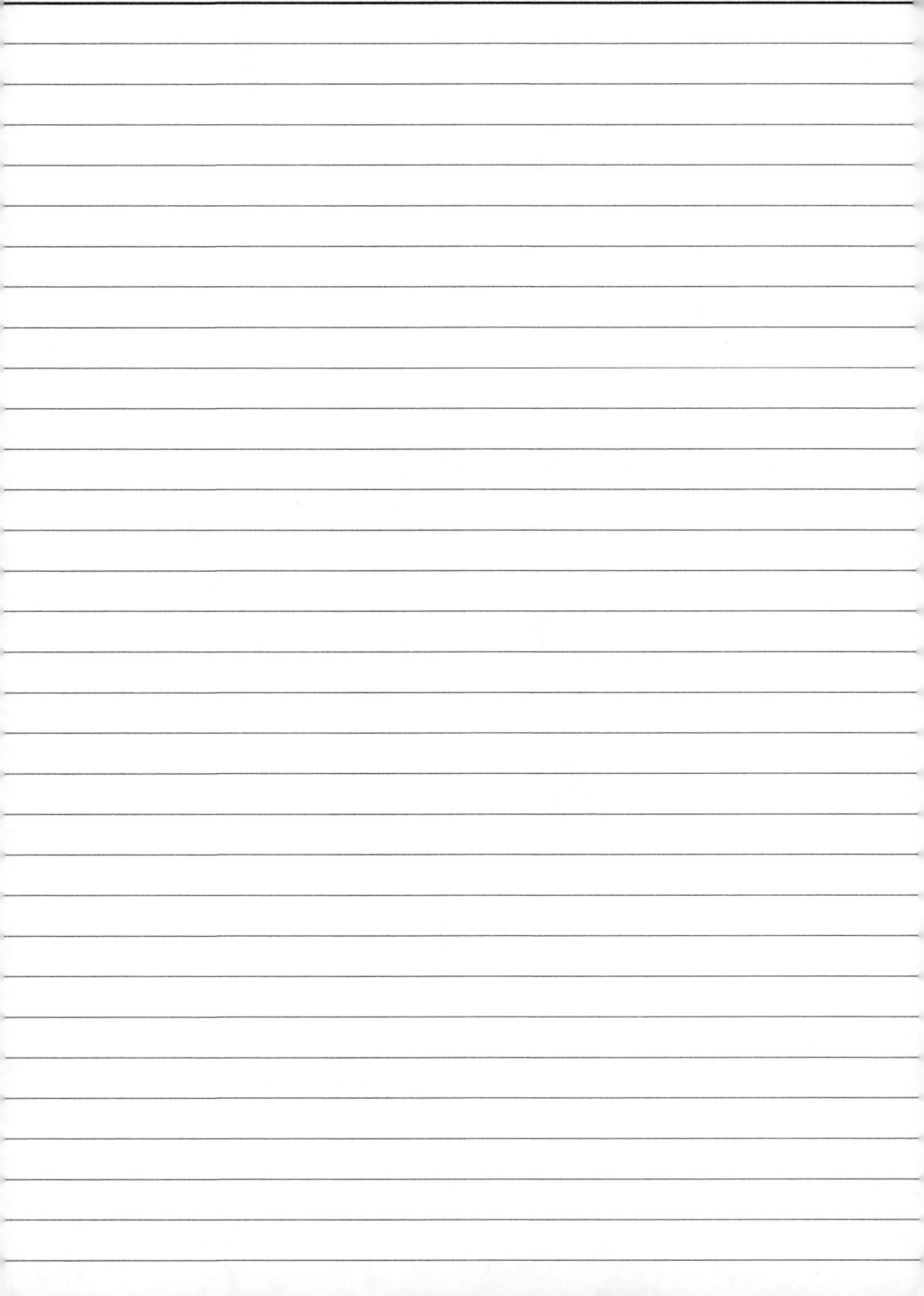

Keep moving forward! You got this!
The journey is just as important as
the destination!!!!

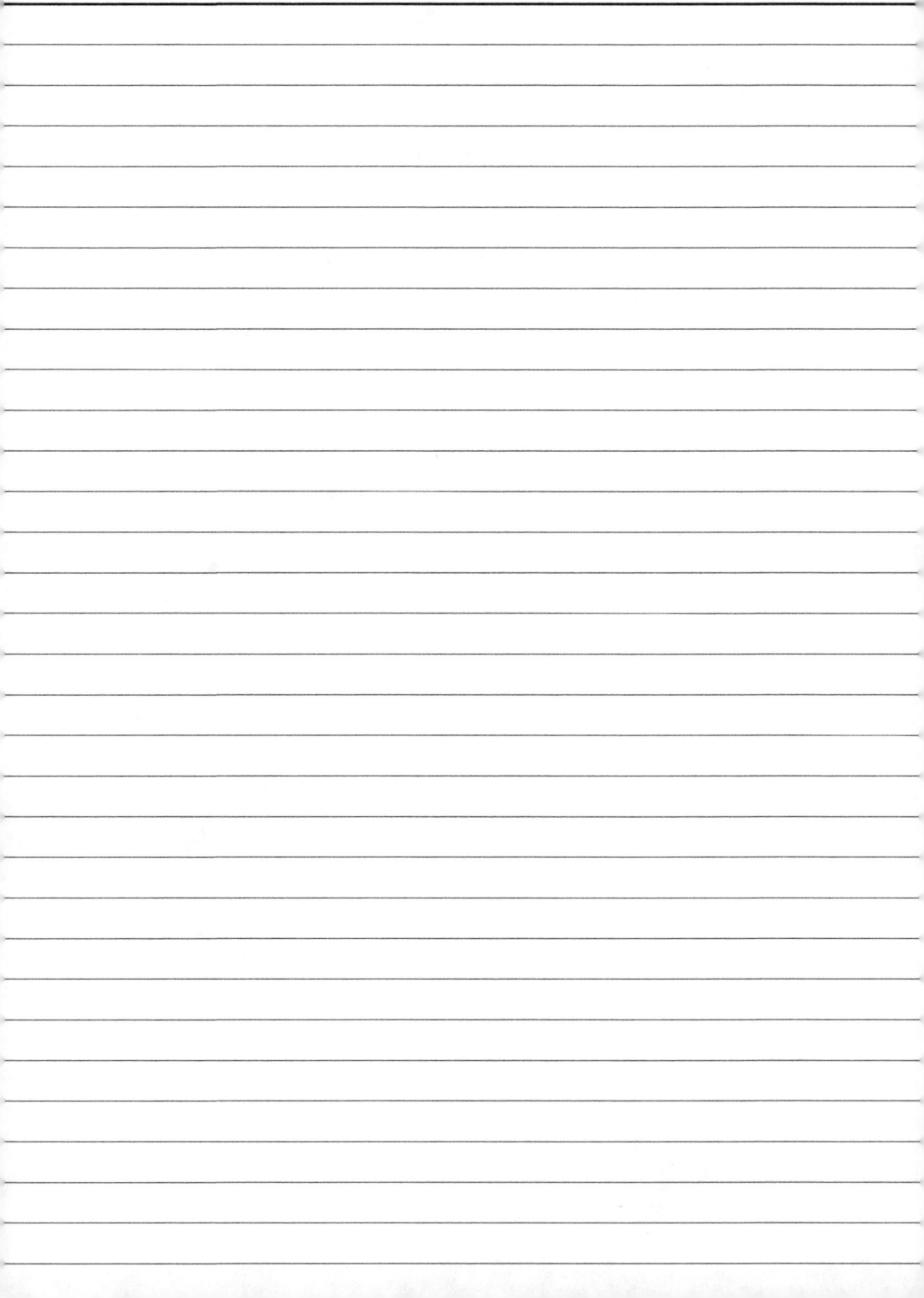

/   /

At every moment encourage yourself.

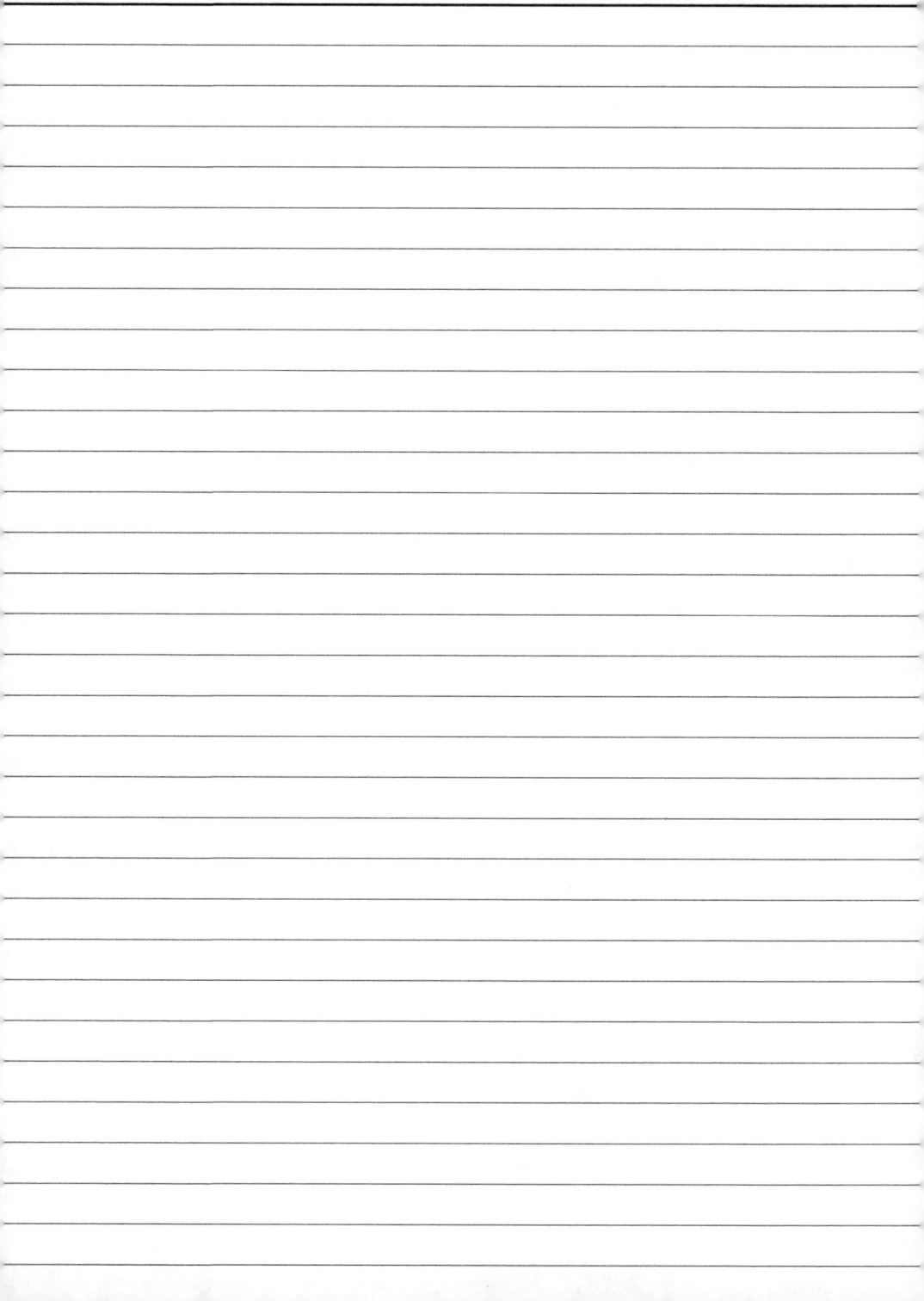

It's time to be happy again.

You're always worth it!

/   /

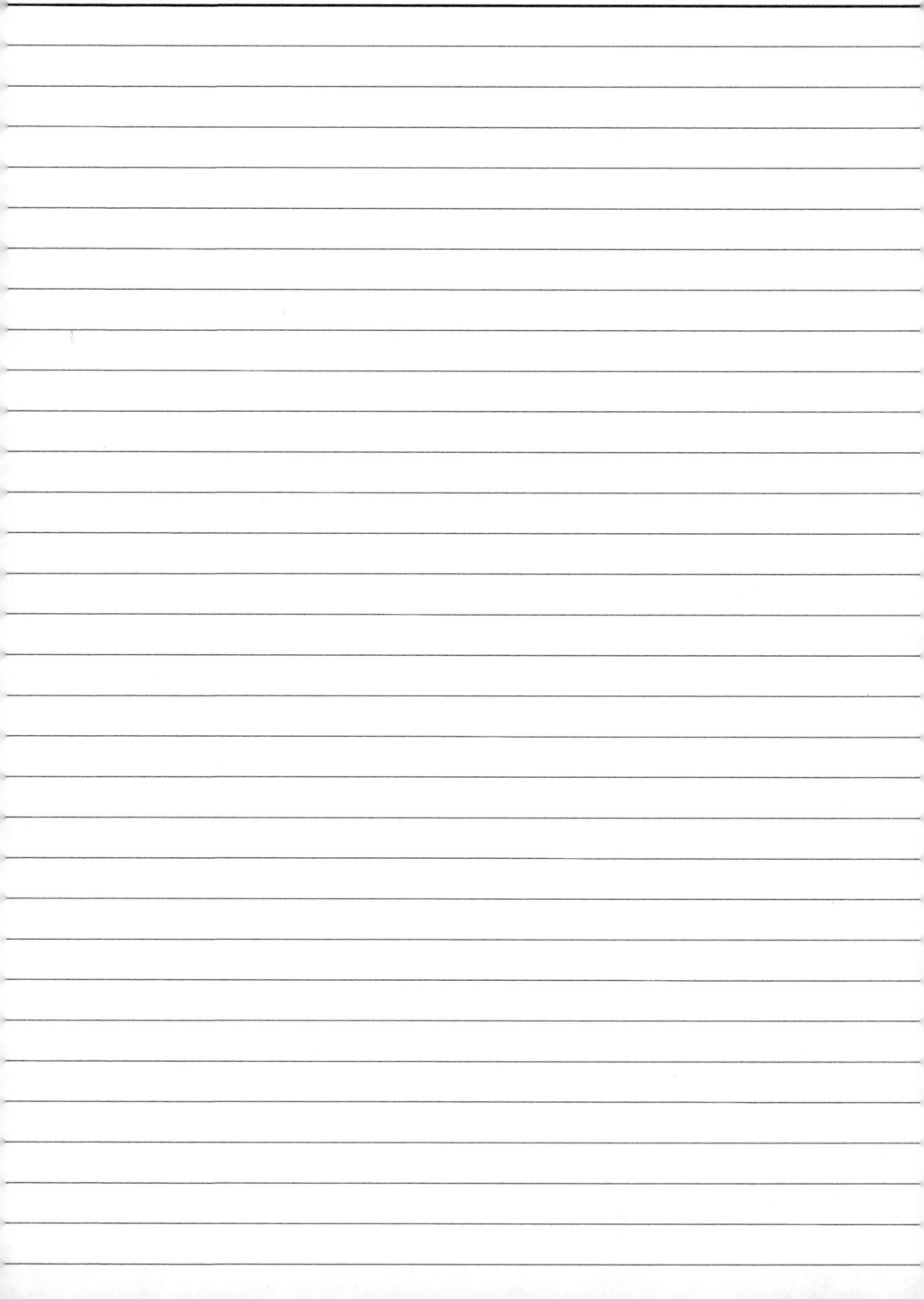

If your dreams don't scare you,
they aren't big enough.

When it comes to your life, you hold the pen.

Find yourself and be yourself.

Create a new mindset that creates new outcomes.

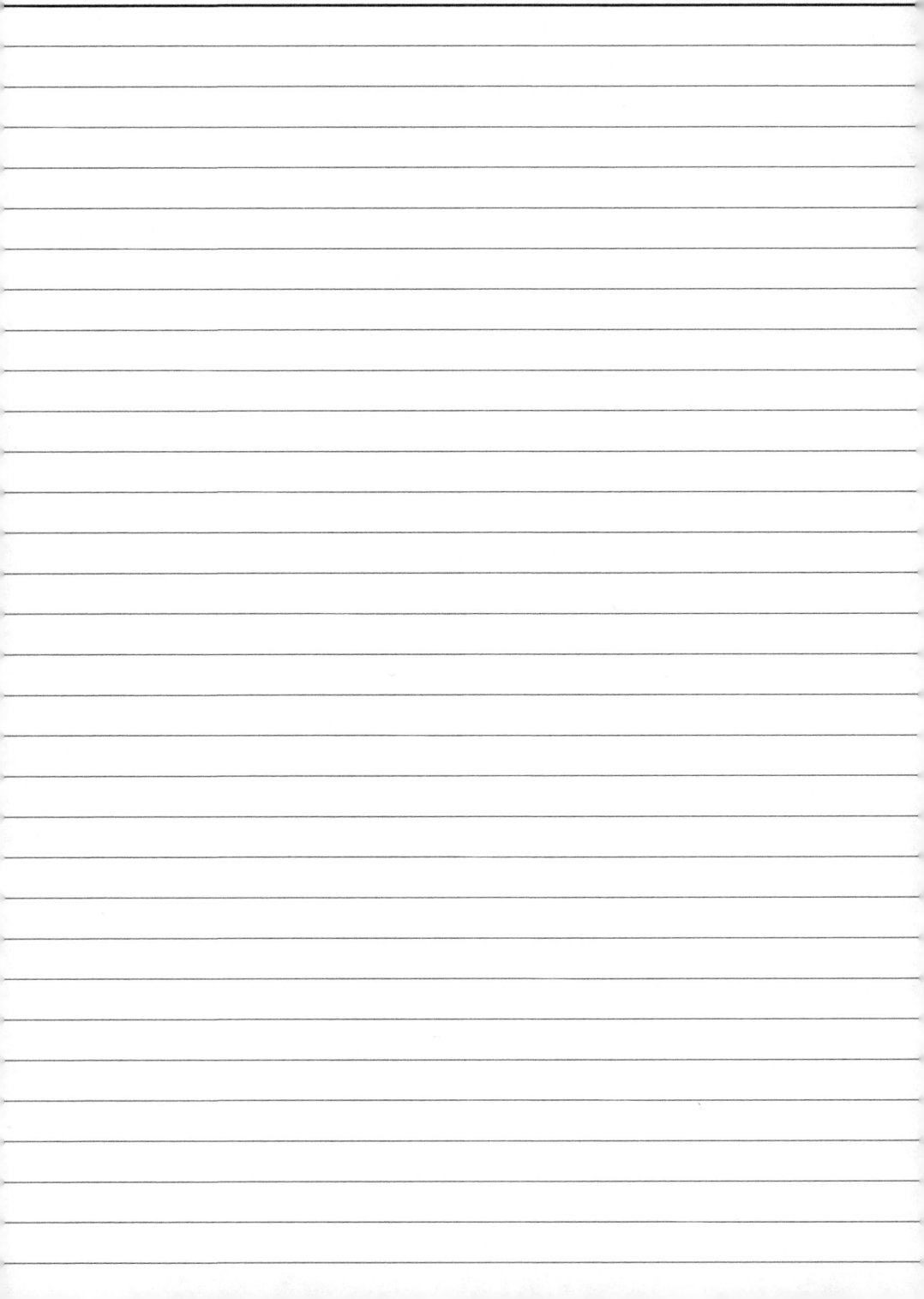

Learn to say no to things that steal your joy.

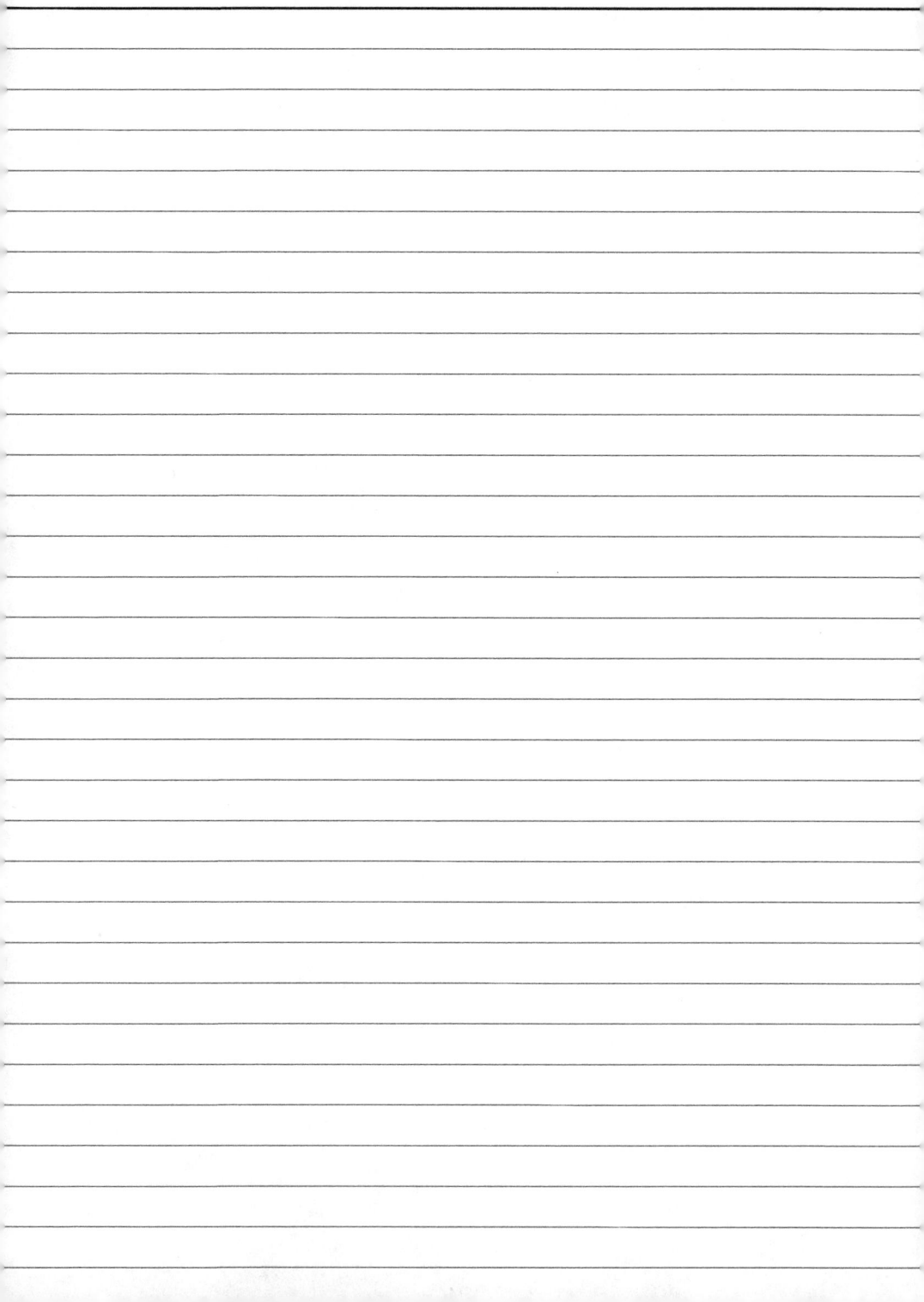

Live like anything is possible.

/ /

Sometimes you just have to let your soul do the talking.

WRITING PROMPT

No more wandering aimlessly. Where did you leave off with your vision board goals? It's time to get your create visual journal out, map out your goals, and make a plan! Let's get to work!!!

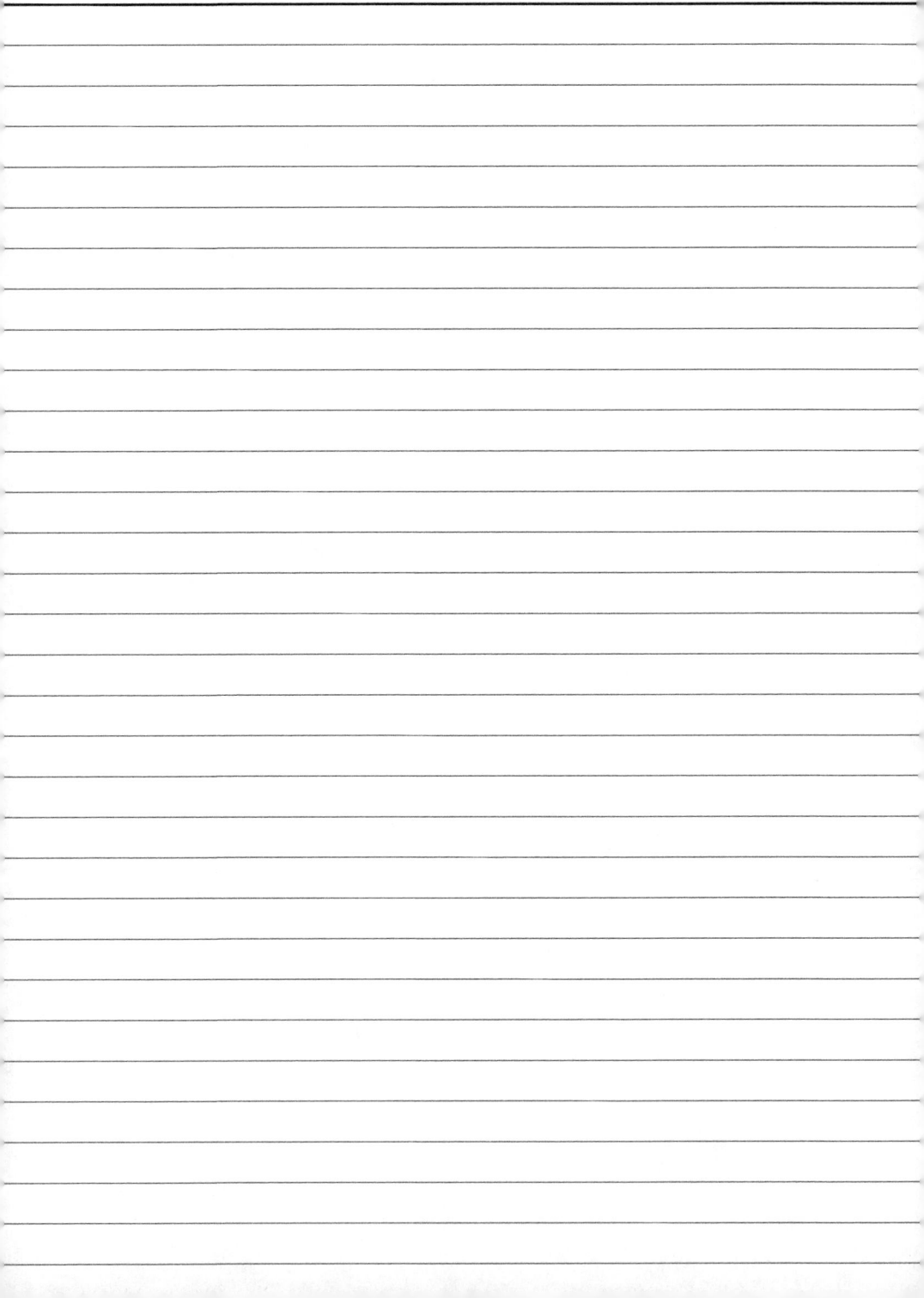

/   /

Sometimes a break in your journey needs to happen in order for a breakthrough to take place.

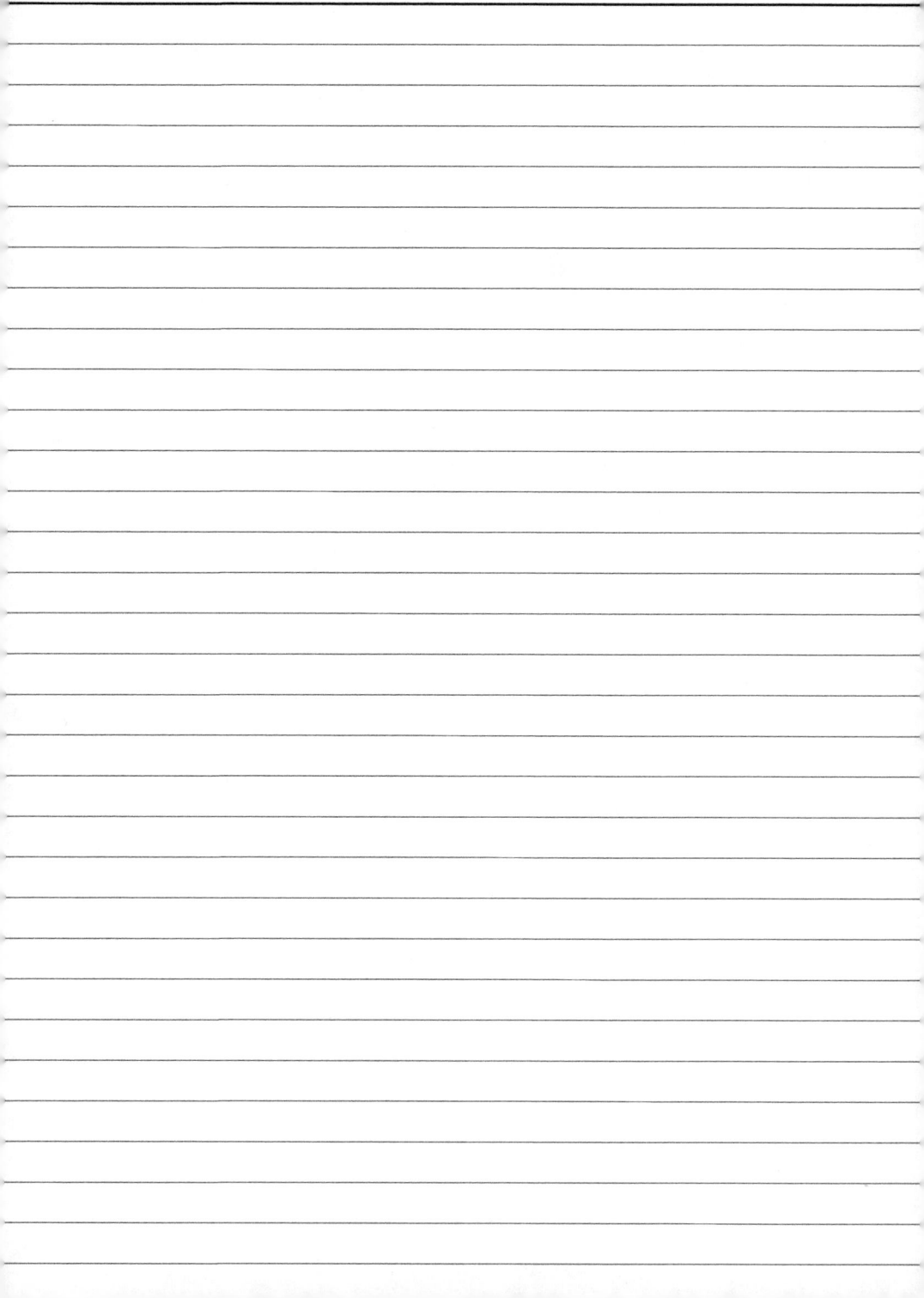

As you pursue your goals, don't forget to enjoy the journey.

/ /

WRITING PROMPT

When do you feel the most comfortable in your own skin?

/ /

"You matter. You are not forgotten. Your voice should be heard." What comes to mind when you read this statement?

WRITING PROMPT

/   /

WRITING PROMPT

Look in the mirror at yourself for a brief moment. When you look in the mirror, what do you see? What do you want to see? What do you want others to see?

/   /

JOURNAL SPACE: How do you like
to spend your time journaling?
Outdoors, a quiet space
with candles, light
music, or etc.

/ /

WRITING PROMPT

What do you love about
what you do for work?
What would you change
to make it better?

WRITING PROMPT

In what ways do you want to feel love from romantic relationships, family, and friends?

/ /

WRITING PROMPT

What song lyrics speak to your heart right now? Write the lyrics and express why these words stand out to you.

/   /

/   /   WRITING PROMPT

"The Best of Me." What do these words mean to you?

WRITING PROMPT

You are beautiful just the way you are. What qualities do you believe make you feel beautiful?

WRITING PROMPT

What are five qualities you love about your personality?

/   /

/   /   Happiness is always an inside job.

/   /

Don't let anyone dull
your shine. Ever.

/   /

Anytime you even think
about giving up. Don't.

/   /

/ /   It's time to be happy again.

WHAT WORDS CANNOT EXPRESS, YOUR HEART SPEAKS.

-Latonia

Art Journaling

www.ingramcontent.com/pod-product-compliance
Lightning Source LLC
Chambersburg PA
CBHW071853090426
42811CB00004B/591